notes on

milton's works

by j. m. evans, m.a., m.ed.

FORUM HOUSE

CONTENTS

... continued

CONTENTS (Continued)

LIFE OF MILTON

First Period — Birth and Parentage: John Milton was born on Friday, December 9th, 1608 (over seven years before the death of Shakespeare). His grandfather, Richard Milton, a landed proprietor in Oxfordshire, was a Roman Catholic, who adhered to his belief, and was fined for refusing to attend his parish church. His son John, the poet's father, became a Protestant. He was driven from home, went to London, and set up as a scrivener. About 1600 he married. He had six children, of whom three died young. Of those who lived, the eldest, Anne, became Mrs. Phillips. The second was the poet, and the third, Christopher Milton, became a judge and was knighted.

Education — Milton the Student: About 1620 he was sent to St. Paul's School as a day scholar. He had also a private tutor, Thomas Young, who became Master of Jesus College, Cambridge. Home influence moulded his character. In his own account of his school life we read: "My father destined me while yet a little boy for the study of humane letters, which I seized with such eagerness that from the twelfth year of my age I scarcely ever went from my lessons to bed before midnight; which, indeed, was the first cause of injury to my eyes, to whose natural weakness there were also added frequent headaches. All which not retarding my impetuosity in learning, he caused me to be daily instructed, both at the grammar school and under other masters at home, and then when I had acquired various tongues, and also not some insignificant taste for the sweetness of philosophy, he sent me to Cambridge."

Milton entered Christ's College, Cambridge, as a student, February 12th, 1624-1625, at the age of 15 years. His matriculation entry is dated April 9th, 1625. Between these two dates James I had died. His University career lasted until July, 1632. In 1626 he had a quarrel with his tutor. In his *Life of Milton* Johnson says that he was one of the last students in the University to receive corporal punishment; Professor Masson says that this story deserves no credit. Milton left College for a time. When he returned, the matter was arranged, he changed his tutor, and did not lose a term through his absence. He took his B.A. degree in January, 1628-1629, and the reputation he gained for scholarship was increased during the remainder of his stay. In July, 1632, he took his M.A. degree and left Cambridge.

His father intended him to enter the Church, but while at Cambridge Milton altered his mind, and on leaving Cambridge he went to reside at Horton, where his father had retired.

Here he "spent a complete holiday over the Greek and Latin Authors", trying to fit himself by labour and study to achieve some great work as a poet.

Travel: To prepare himself for his great work, he determined to see other lands and other men. His father supplied the money for expenses, and in 1638 he set out for the Continent. The last news before he left England was that the Scottish Covenant had been made.

He visited Paris, and went to Italy by way of Nice. After visiting Genoa, Leghorn and Pisa, he arrived at Florence in August, 1638. There he visited the great Galileo, then old and blind, and nominally a prisoner to the Inquisition for his astronomical heresy. From Florence he went to Rome, and spent about two months visiting the galleries, ruins and antiquities. He mixed both at Rome and at Florence with the most learned men of the day, and formed friends there. From Rome he went on to Naples. There he heard of Civil War breaking out in England, and determined to give up his self-indulgent life and return to aid in the fight for liberty, instead of visiting Sicily and Greece as he intended. Finding the news rather exaggerated, he spent some time on the return journey, and arrived in England, August, 1639.

Second Period — Milton the Publicist and State Official: So far Milton's life had been one of quiet secluded study. For the next twenty years study and self-preparation were given up, and he was engaged in the great controversies of the day.

He settled in a house in Aldersgate Street (his father had left Horton to live with his other son), and took charge of the education of his nephews (the Phillips) and others joining in their lessons; he had quite a school.

In 1643 he was again in the country, and returned with a young wife, Mary Powell. They were unsuited for each other, for she was only 17 and he was 35; she could not enter into his lofty aims and aspirations, and in a few months she asked to be allowed to visit her home. On her promise to return in a month or so, Milton let her go, but when the time came she would not return. This caused some of his writings concerning *Divorce,* which gained him the ill-will of all Churchmen. As her father was a Royalist and Milton a strong Parliamentarian, her father sanctioned her absence.

In 1645, however, the king's cause was ruined at Naseby, and her family wishing to be friends with so powerful a man as Milton, some friends effected a reconciliation, and he took the protection of her family in hand, her parents staying with them while there was danger to them as Royalists.

She remained with him until her death, in 1652, and of her four children three daughters were left.

In 1649 the Council of State, who were practically the rulers of the country, wanted a Latin Secretary to translate the foreign despatches, as Latin was the language employed in the written diplomatic documents.

The office was offered to Milton, partly on account of his scholarly attainments and partly on account of his fearless method of writing against what he considered abuses. Thinking to serve the cause of liberty thereby, he accepted it, although his eyesight was threatened. During this period of office, he wrote a number of pamphlets on various themes, in defence of the action of the Republican Government. Although warned that he was destroying his eyesight, he refused to relinquish "a supreme duty", and in 1652 he became totally blind. An assistant was appointed to help in his official duties. In November, 1656, he married Catherine Woodcock, who died early in 1658. This short period was one of the happiest parts of his domestic life, and he expressed his grief for her death in one of his finest Sonnets.

After the death of Cromwell, the Republican Government soon ended, and in 1660 Charles II was proclaimed King.

Third Period — Milton in Retirement: How Milton escaped the scaffold at the Restoration is a great marvel. He must have had some powerful friends at Court, as many of the Royalists had marked him out for a special punishment on account of his writings. However, by some means or other he was not excluded from the benefits of *The Indemnity Bill,* and could walk freely again without fear of arrest, such as had caused him to keep in hiding when danger was threatening.

After the Restoration he lived in Holborn, but soon removed to Jewin Street. He had lost a large sum of money, and was not so well off as formerly. His daughters were far from kind to him, and at length were sent out to learn embroidery.

On the advice of Dr. Paget, he married a third wife, Elizabeth Minshull, who kept her house and her husband "excellently well". He then went to live in Bunhill Row, where he spent the remainder of his life (except a few months in 1665, during the plague, when he went to Chalfont St. Giles, in Bucks). Here he completed his greatest poem, *Paradise Lost*. On the publication of this, his great merits were recognised, and many visited him, including Dryden.

Some of his friends who had adhered to him during his period of adversity after the Restoration were Thomas Ellwood, Dr. Paget and Edward Phillips (his nephew).

Death: Gout was hereditary in his case, and he peacefully passed away during an attack of "gout struck in" on Sunday, November 8th, 1674, and was buried the following Thursday, in St. Giles' Church, Cripplegate, a very large concourse of people being present at the funeral.

MILTON'S CHIEF WORKS

1. PROSE WORKS

1641. *Of Reformation touching Church Discipline in England and the causes that have hitherto hindered it.*

1642. *An Apology for Smectymnuus.* Five Presbyterian ministers, Stephen Marshall, Edmund Calamy, Thomas Young (Milton's former tutor), Matthew Newcomen and William Spurston, had written an attack on Church government. Their initials form the word *Smectymnuus.*

1644. *A Tractate on Education.*

1644. *Areopagitica.* A fine work advocating Freedom of the Press.

1644-5. *The Doctrine and Practice of Divorce.* Five pamphlets on this subject were written.

1649. *Eikonoklastes* (The image breaker). This was an answer to *Eikon Basilike* (The royal image), a book of prayers and meditations said to have been written by Charles I.

1651. *Defensio pro Populo Anglicano.* In this he defended the execution of the King.

1654. *Defensio Secunda.*

1670. *History of Britain.* Milton completed only as far as the Conquest.

His *Treatise on Christian Doctrine* was not published until 1825. Macaulay's *Essay on Milton* was a review of this book.

2. POETICAL WORKS

Earlier Poems

1629. *Ode on the Nativity.*

1633. *L'Allegro* and *Il Penseroso*. One describes the cheerful man, and the other the pensive, meditative man.

1633. *Arcades*. A portion of a Masque given before the Countess Dowager of Derby, at Harefield, by some noble members of her family.

1634. *Comus*. A Masque presented at Ludlow Castle before the Earl of Bridgwater, Lord President of Wales.

1637. *Lycidas*. An Elegy on the death of Edward King, who was drowned on the passage from Chester to Ireland.

Later Poems

1667. *Paradise Lost*. The greatest poem in the English language.

1671. *Paradise Regained*. A sequel to *Paradise Lost*.

1671. *Samson Agonistes* (The wrestler).

In addition to these he wrote a number of *Sonnets, Odes* and other minor poems.

Milton's Latin Poems

Milton's Latin poetry is especially valuable in tracing the development of his literary and philosophic perspectives during his early years at the University and at Horton. Most of these poems are elegies, modelled after those of the Roman elegists. Milton imitates rather closely the ornate manner of Ovid, or, later, the dignified restraint of Virgil. Some classical scholars consider his Latin verse the finest ever written by an English poet. Writing in Latin, however, was for Milton only an exercise in composition and discipline — a warm-up for ultimate expression in his native language.

Elegy I expresses the poet's satisfaction with his cultural way of life in London, as well as with the simple, sensuous pleasures of daily living. The form of the poem is definitely Ovidian, and mythological allusions abound amid the elegant Latin numbers. In *Elegy II* Milton emphasizes quite strongly the element of romantic love. *Elegy IV* is addressed to his tutor, Thomas Young, for whom he expresses devout loyalty, and *Elegy VII* shows the hold that Cupid has over him. While in other elegies Milton writes of love, yet does not succumb, here he belabors the fact that he is a victim. In *Elegy V* (the chronology is not definitely known) Milton sings of springtime and its beauties. It is full of imagery of an erotic nature, abounding in pagan revelry. *Elegy VI* is a break in the indulgence in frankness and sensuousness. He is dissatisfied with writing easy, trifling verses; he longs to write epic poetry, and in the future he vows to Diodati, his friend that he will live like an ascetic and dedicate himself to lofty ideals and behavior befitting an epic poet.

His best Latin poem, perhaps, is his *Epitaphium Damonis,* a pastoral elegy that celebrates his friendship with Diodati. This poem, written about 1640, is full of tenderness and has about it a depth and warmth of feeling that Milton rarely achieved later. It is not to be compared with *Lycidas,* however, in other qualities: dignity, elevation of thought, and varied moods. In the poem he passes from an apotheosis of his friend to a consecration of himself to spiritual values which his friend, now gone, had inspired in him. He laments the fact that no longer will he be able to share with him all his poetic ambitions and achievements. Diodati becomes an immortal soul righteously rewarded.

Beside the elegies, Milton wrote poems in other forms, like the one on the Gunpowder Plot, a poem of epic proportions describing the plan of Satan against King James as a punishment to England because of its refusal to obey him (Satan). Here can be found elements used later in *Paradise Lost.* Also this poem shows Milton fanatically Protestant in the best traditions of his religious party.

The Italian Poems

Milton used still another medium to express himself, the Italian of his favorite authors. They are sonnets and canzone written, probably, in his academic years, and not when he travelled to Italy. They are not so polished or ingenious as the Latin verses. The sonnets are conventional in theme and manner. They deal with the punishments that Cupid or Love heap upon him for not succumbing to the allurements of love. The language is flowery, cavalier, and deliberately subtle in concealing the name of the lady, Emilia. Again, Diodati is addressed often, and Milton follows the tradition of Petrarchan sonnet-writing rather slavishly.

COMMENTS ON MILTON'S WORKS

In his *Essay on Milton* Macaulay says, "It is to be regretted that the prose writings of Milton should, in our time, be so little read. As compositions they deserve the attention of every man who wishes to become acquainted with the full power of the English language. They abound with passages compared with which the finest declamations of Burke sink into insignificance. They are a perfect field of cloth of gold. The style is stiff with gorgeous embroidery. Not even in the earlier books of *Paradise Lost* has the great poet ever risen higher then in those parts of his controversial works in which his feelings, excited by conflict, find a vent in bursts of devotional and lyric rapture. It is, to borrow his own majestic language, 'a sevenfold chorus of hallelujahs and harping symphonies'."

The same writer says of his Poetry, "His poetry acts like an incantation. Its merit lies less in its obvious meaning than in its occult power. There would seem at first sight to be no more in his words than in other words. No sooner are they pronounced, than the past is present and the distant near. New forms of beauty start at once into existence, and all the burial-places of the memory give up their dead. Change the structure of the sentence; substitute one synonym for another, and the whole effect is destroyed. The spell loses its power; and he who should then hope to conjure with it would find himself as much mistaken as Cassim in the Arabian tale, when he stood crying 'Open Wheat,' 'Open Barley,' to the door, which obeyed no sounds but 'Open Sesame'. The miserable failure of Dryden in his attempt to translate into his own diction some parts of the *Paradise Lost* is a remarkable example of this."

OUTLINES OF MILTON'S POEMS AND SONNETS

AN EPITAPH ON THE MARCHIONESS OF WINCHESTER

Lady Jane, wife of John Paulet, after her death in child birth, was responsible for this tender eulogy. Again we have the octosyllabic couplet, and the style and manner are of the Jonsonian school.

ARCADES

Arcades is a brief masque, in honor of the Countess Dowager of Derby, suggested by Henry Lawes, a musician, who probably performed the role of the Genius of the Wood. The masque is a dramatic entertainment involving disguises, dances, and spectacular scenic and musical effects. Plot and characterization are submerged in importance. The actors of this hodge-podge of music, dancing, staging, drama, and spectacle usually were amateurs popular with the sovereigns of the day at court. Some of the best masque writers were Chapman, Middleton, Jonson, and Beaumont, and the greatest scene designer and architect was Inigo Jones.

Milton's *Arcades* is a slight piece without much plot. A group of shepherds sing a complimentary song to the lady they have searched for, their Arcadian queen who happens to be the same person in whose honor the entertainment is presented. Then enters the Genius of the Wood, who addresses her and brings her to the Arcadians, singing the lovely song, "O'er the smooth enamelled green."

A dance follows and final lyric ends the masque. The poetic qualities are of the same kind we find in *L'Allegro* and *Il Penseroso*. Again the image of the music of the spheres is used. The address of the Genius of the Wood is in decasyllabic couplets.

AT A SOLEMN MUSIC

The theme of this inspired ode is immortality, and Milton here speaks of the Platonic idea of the music of the spheres. Voice and verse are sisters. The mood is religious, mystical, meditative.

AT A VACATION EXERCISE

Expresses Milton's ambition to write epic poetry. He celebrates also his own language as a fit medium for lofty poetry. He uses the heroic couplet. Sections of this poem have the later Miltonic accent of sublimity.

CAPTAIN, OR COLONEL, OR KNIGHT AT ARMS

The occasion for this sonnet is the advance of the Royalist cavalry on London after the battle of Edgehill. Milton compares himself to Pindar who also had penned a poem on the door so that the enemy could spare the place. Note the bare style and harsh tones.

COMUS

THE AUTOBIOGRAPHY IN "COMUS"

After leaving Cambridge in 1632 Milton lived in retirement for six years at Horton, near Windsor, studying Greek, Roman, Italian and English literatures. All these have left their imprint on the masque which he wrote at the age of 25. The general effect of this period of calm and peaceful retirement is obvious too in the quietude of many parts of the poem. His love for Purity, Chastity, and Temperance is clearly shown, and his feeling that there would be a downfall of the Court Party.

Milton shows his own character in the personages of the poem. The lofty bearing of the lady with a touch of austerity is his own reaction to temptation; the didactic tone adopted by the elder brother in his insistence that Virtue will always be triumphant is an echo of the younger poet's own thoughts.

His friendship with Charles Diodati, whom he had known since boyhood and who died while Milton was enjoying his Continental journey, is illustrated by the lines:—

> He loved me well, and oft would beg me sing
> Which when I did, he on the tender grass
> Would sit, and hearken even to ecstacy;
> And in requital ope his leathern scrip,
> And show me simples of a thousand names,
> Telling their strange and vigorous faculties.

> (Lines 623-628)

It was to Charles that Milton confided his poetic ambitions, and he probably read some of his earliest efforts also to this friend; Charles, in return, doubtless imparted to Milton some of his medical knowledge.

His love for music is shown throughout the masque; vocal and instrumental music delighted him especially in his early years, and both his father and Henry Lawes encouraged this love for music.

In his youth, too, he would certainly have seen groups of country dancers, such as he suggests enjoyed themselves in the grounds of Ludlow Castle.

His reading of Plato and Homer, of Ovid, of Spenser and Shakespeare, of Fletcher and Browne is well illustrated in *Comus* by his reminiscences of the works of these writers.

THE ORIGIN AND MEANING OF "COMUS"

Comus, the most important of Milton's early poems is a masque, that is a form of entertainment which in the reigns of Elizabeth and James I took to a certain extent the part taken by our modern opera. It had a slight element of story, but relied for its effect chiefly upon pageantry and songs, splendid dresses and gorgeous scenery. The masque really came from Italy; it was one of the entertainments connected with the Italian Carnival. It is suggested that masques were known in England from the time of Edward III, but it was in the sixteenth and seventeenth centuries that they became extremely popular. The early mystery-plays became more elaborate, and some elements of the Greek drama were added to raise these entertainments to a higher educational level. At Court festivals they were much in vogue and such writers as Beaumont, Fletcher, Ben Jonson, William Browne, Dekker, Shirley and Carew utilised their talents in producing interesting and spectacular masques. The lawyers at the Inns of Court, too, used much money in producing elaborate masques, and when they spent a large amount on the production of Shirley's *Triumph of Peace,* the courtiers at the palace of Whitehall vied with them by showing Carew's *Coelum Britannicum.* In the third decade of the seventeenth century the Puritan element in England was becoming very strong, and Prynne wrote *Histriomastix* against stage plays. This, however, had with various sections of the community an influence different from that which he intended; there was a sudden revival of interest in plays and especially in masques. The marvellous masques of Ben Jonson who had usually worked in collaboration with the great architect Inigo Jones, were revived, and other writers copied their magnificence. Milton wrote *Arcades* as part of an entertainment presented to the Countess Dowager of Derby by some of the younger members of her family; and though this was slight and experimental it embodied the main features of a masque.

In 1634 the Earl of Bridgewater, the stepson of the Countess of Derby, went formally to Ludlow Castle to take up his position as Lord Lieutenant of the Welsh Marches, and it was proposed that an entertainment should be given to welcome him. The most obvious suggestion was the performance of the masque, and Henry Lawes, the music-master of the Earl's children suggested to his friend John Milton that they should collaborate in one, Milton writing the words and Lawes the music. This was agreed upon, with the result that *Comus* was performed at Ludlow Castle on Michaelmas Day, September 29th, 1634. Lawes himself took the part of the Attendant Spirit, and the three children of the Earl, Lady Alice Egerton aged 14, Viscount Brackley aged 12, and Mr. Thomas Egerton aged 10, were the chief performers. Milton did not give a name to the work but called it simply "A Mask." It was obviously a great success because Henry Lawes had frequent requests for copies. In 1637 the work was published, not by the poet himself, but by Henry Lawes, who must, however, have gained Milton's consent for he states in the dedication to Viscount Brackley, *Although not openly acknowledged by the author, yet it is a legitimate offspring, so lovely and so much desired, that the often copying of it hath tired my pen to give my several friends satisfaction.* In 1645 Milton himself published the masque together with some of his early poems; he included the dedication Lawes had written in 1637 and also a eulogistic letter written by Sir Henry Wotton praising *the dainty piece of entertainment* and adding *I should much commend the tragical part if the lyrical did not ravish me with a certain Doric delicacy in your songs and odes, whereunto I*

must plainly confess to have seen yet nothing parallel in our language.
In the eighteenth century the title *Comus* was applied to this work.

Comus differs from many other masques in its meaning and its form. It has to some extent a political significance since it upholds the Puritan virtues — Purity, Chastity and Temperance, and condemns the licence and spirit of corruption of the Court party. Purity is shown in opposition to gross Pleasure, and the conflict between them, Milton suggests, is continual. This does not mean that the poem is a depressing one; it is, really, the happiest that Milton ever wrote, but the happiness, instead of being a light-hearted variety is grave and serene. Virtue is not shown merely as a duty; it is worshipped as a delight. The underlying thought is the probation which every soul must undergo, and from which it will emerge triumphant if it follows the path of Virtue.

Contrary to most masques, the speeches are more important than the songs, and these speeches are weighty with profound moral truths. Still the element of song *is* present, and dancing is introduced, and the masque certainly gains, by these means, in lightness and grace. In the early masques it was common for revels to take place, that is, dancing in which those acting tripped around with the onlookers during one part of the performance, and there was generally an anti-masque too in which ludicrous dancers were introduced. There is dancing in *Comus,* beautiful and also clumsy or even grotesque. The anti-masque is represented by the clumsy movement of the country dancers just before the Attendant Spirit brings in the lost children, and by the grotesque antics of the followers of Comus who were probably represented as rushing about on the stage in semi-darkness.

The meaning of the word *Comus* is *revel* (Greek Kōmos). The Greek word was applied to a procession which took place at regular intervals in honour of Dionysius (the Latin *Bacchus*) the god of wine. These processions sometimes became very unruly so the name *Comus* became associated with a being who encouraged riotous revels.

MILTON'S DEBT TO OTHER WRITERS

For the actual story of *Comus* Milton was probably most greatly indebted to the *Old Wives' Tale* of George Peele, a work published in 1595, which tells how a lady was carried away from Thessaly to Britain by a sorcerer called Sacrapant. Through his arts he is able to change her shape, and when her brothers find her they are made into his slaves. Eventually her lover, through the help of the spirit of a friend who has died, is able to rescue the lady and her brothers.

Some of the details are used in their exactitude by Milton, but the literary merits of *Comus* are greatly above those of its prototype.

Milton also probably took a number of his details from John Fletcher's *Faithful Shepherdess,* a play which was produced in 1610. The Attendant Spirit, the Lady, the use of a herb, the invoking of a river-spirit are all found in Fletcher's work, and it is moreover, connected with the rescue of a heroine whose chastity is in danger. It is interesting to note that Fletcher's play was acted at a London theatre in 1633.

In 1634 too, a reprint was made of a Latin play called *Comus* which had been written by a professor of the University of Louvain, named Puteanus in 1608. It is possible that Milton adapted some details from this and also borrowed the name.

The idea of making the Lady the representative of Purity and Chastity may have originated from a reading of Spenser's *Faerie Queene* and the connection of Una and Britomart with these virtues, and from Spenser too may have been taken the episode of Sabrina. For the details of this, however, it seems more probable that Milton was indebted to the work of a Welsh historian, Geoffrey of Monmouth, who lived in the twelfth century, for we know that the Puritan poet was well acquainted with this treatise.

A character named *Comus* appears in a masque of Ben Jonson's *Pleasure reconciled to Virtue;* though the two masques are quite unlike, the resemblance of the name and the basic idea is worth noting.

Some resemblances too can be traced to Shakespeare's *Midsummer Night's Dream,* and *Tempest,* and probably much of the literature that Milton had read was instrumental in suggesting details to the poet. Nevertheless *Comus* is not just an agglomeration of other stories; it is a product of the poet's own imagination based on a foundation of earlier drama and myth.

In all Milton's work there are no references to Greek and Latin literature and to that produced by earlier English writers such as Spenser and Shakespeare, but this is quite natural owing to the poet's wide reading. Like Spenser, Milton went to the writings of Plato for the respresentation of his ideas concerning the virtue of Chastity. In the *Phaedo* of Plato there are various references to the soul being made immortal by dwelling in thought on matters connected with purity, and the opposite suggestion is also frequently made, viz. that impure thoughts defile the soul and make it become entirely carnal.

This is the argument employed by the Elder Brother in Lines 453-475. Typical lines in this connection are the following:—

> Oft converse with heavenly habitants
> Begin to cast a beam on the outward shape,
> The unpolluted temple of the mind,
> And turns it by degrees to the soul's essence,
> Till all be made immortal.
>
> (Lines 459-463)

> The soul grows clotted by contagion
> Imbodies and imbrutes, till she quite lose
> The divine property of her first being.
>
> (Lines 467-469)

Platonic influence is seen too in the epithet *divine* applied to *philosophy*: — *How charming is divine philosophy* (Line 476), and in the eulogy of the Chastity and the inability of the impure even to realise the beauty of the virtue:—

> Thou hast not ear, not soul, to apprehend
> The sublime notion, and high mystery,
> That must be uttered to unfold the sage
> And serious doctrine of Virginity.
>
> (Lines 784-787)

Innumerable references to the myths of Greece and Rome are given and classical influence is obvious too in words and phrases. (For details see *notes on the texts* and the remarks on *Milton's style and diction*).

Spenserian influence is shown in (i) the instances of archaic language, (ii) the use of abstract for concrete terms, e.g.

> If your stray attendance be yet lodged.
>
> (Line 315)

(iii) some of the nature descriptions such as:—

> huge forests and unharboured heaths,
> Infamous hills, and sandy perilous wilds.
>
> (Lines 423 and 424)

(iv) the pastoral ideas:—

> this have I learnt
> Tending my flocks hard by i' the hilly crofts
> That brow the bottom glade.
>
> (Lines 530-532)

(v) actual reminiscences of the *Faerie Queene* such as:—

> Refreshments after toil, ease after pain.
>
> (Line 687)

and (vi) the allegory that is the integral part of the masque. Shakespeare as well as Spencer may be responsible for some of Milton's Elizabethan diction such as,

> Yet some there be.   (Line 12)

and reminiscences of the great dramatist can be found throughout *Comus* not only in the use of blank verse varied by rhyming couplets and by songs, but also in definite phrases. Thus *Hail, foreign wonder* (Line 265) brings to one's mind immediately Ferdinand's words in *The Tempest,* and the lines:—

> What need a man forestall his date of grief
> And run to meet what he would most avoid?
>
> (Lines 362 and 363)

are very like the sentiments expressed in a soliloquy in *Hamlet.* Again we are forcibly reminded of the lovely song *I know a bank whereon the wild thyme blows* in the *Midsummer Night's Dream* by Milton's lines:—

> I sat me down to watch upon a bank
> With ivy canopied, and interwove
> With flaunting honeysuckle.
>
> (Lines 543-545)

At the time that Milton was writing, certain other poets had begun to adopt a style of verse that was full of farfetched similes. Such poets were called Metaphysical; it is noticeable however, that Milton had very little in common with them though he shared their delight in Personification. Here is just a passage in *Comus* that can be considered a little metaphysical; it is the simile describing the dark:—

> Why should'st thou, but for some felonious end,
> In thy dark lanthorn thus close up the stars
> That nature hung in heaven, and filled their lamps
> With everlasting oil, to give due light
> To the misled and lonely traveller.
>
> (Lines 196-200)

Whatever Milton took from other poets, however, was transmuted by his genius, and partook of his own individual power; it was not *merely* a borrowing; thus from a very uninteresting passage taken from an early Elizabethan writer — Purchas — in a book called *Abstract of Marco Polo* Milton has evolved these wonderful lines:—

> A thousand fantasies
> Begin to throng into my memory,
> Of calling shapes and beckoning shadows dire,
> And airy tongues, that syllable men's names
> On sands and shores and desert wildernesses.
>
> (Lines 205-209)

EXPLANATION OF DIFFICULT PASSAGES

Lines 24 and 25. Because he wished to show favour to those gods who served under him he allowed them to have separate islands to govern.

Lines 36-39. Their way lies through the intricate paths of this gloomy wood in which the dark overhanging branches of the trees seem to threaten the lost wandering traveller.

Lines 88-91. Who is as faithful as he is skilful and is most likely to be out of doors watching his flocks just now and therefore would be the nearest at hand to give the help that is wanted at the present time.

Line 126. It is in daylight that sin is revealed.

Lines 195-200. Why did you, O thief, hide the stars in your dark lantern by closing the shutters on them, when according to Nature their lamps should shine brightly to lighten the way of travellers.

Lines 256 and 257. Who, as they sang, would take the soul prisoner and wrap it up in bliss.

Lines 316-318. I shall know before dawn or before the lark that has roosted on the ground rises from her nest.

Lines 353-358. Perhaps some chilly bank is her pillow now, or perhaps she, filled with sadness and fear, leans her head without any support against the rough bark of an elm-tree. She may be in terrible fear, or even now, while we are speaking, she may be suffering from terrible hunger or heat.

Lines 359-366. Be silent, brother; don't search too closely in your mind to imagine types of danger which may not exist at all; even if such dangers *do* exist there is no need to anticipate a grief that may come to one, and run to meet trouble. If such alarms prove to have been quite unnecessary, you have deluded yourself and suffered bitterness without cause.

Lines 398-407. You may as well spread the heap of treasure, which a miner has formerly kept concealed, in front of the cave of a robber and tell me it is perfectly safe, as suggest to me the hope that Danger will connive at Opportunity and let a maiden be safe in her helplessness in this rough place. I am not worried about the night or the loneliness; what I fear are the terrors that accompany these in the form of greetings from infamous men who may try to harm our solitary sister.

Lines 447-452. What was the Gorgon shield with its snaky lock which the chaste virgin Minerva carried, and by which she was able to petrify her enemies, except the firm austere appearance and her noble mien which caused brutish violence to be overthrown and changed into feelings of adoration and dread.

Lines 555-560. At last a sweet and solemn song arose like perfume on the air so that even Silence fell under the charm before she realised it, and wished that she had *not* to be silent, but could cease to exist if such sounds could for ever take her place.

Lines 589-599. Virtue may be attacked but never harmed; it may be taken unawares but cannot be enslaved; and even those wrongs which mischievous people intended to be most hurtful shall really turn to a glorious victory for the opponents of such mischief; but evil which now is allowed to mix with goodness shall not always do so but shall be gathered separately; it will be like refuse, settling in its own part, feeding on itself and consuming itself; if this is not so the world itself cannot exist; it has no support, no foundation.

Lines 642-647. I placed it in my wallet but did not think about it until compelled to do so by this great difficulty; now, however, I realise that what I was told of it is true; for by this means I recognised the wicked magician in spite of his disguise, entered into the circle of his influence, and yet suffered no harm.

Lines 659-662. Sit, lady; if I just wave this wand your nerves will be quite chained as if in alabaster, and you will be like a statue or like Daphne, when she ran away from Apollo, held fast to the earth as if with roots.

Lines 679-689. Why are you so cruel to yourself and to your beautiful body which was lent you by Nature to be used gently and kindly. You are reversing the conditions of this loan, and dealing like a poor borrower, in a harsh manner with the loan which you received on different terms; you scorn the natural conditions with which all mortals must comply, viz. that they must have refreshment when they have worked, comfort when they have suffered pain, for you have had no food all day, you are tired, you have lost your rest — and yet refuse such comfort and refreshment.

Lines 706-709. Oh, foolish men — who listen to those who by their gowns proclaim themselves Stoics and who, following the doctrines of the Cynics, praise Abstinence which causes people to become thin and unhealthy-looking.

Lines 710-714. Why did Nature bestow such good gifts with such full and generous hands, placing fruits and flocks on the earth and fish in the sea except to please and satisfy fastidious taste.

Lines 730-736. The earth would be overburdened and the air made dark by the wings of great multitudes of birds, the flocks would be greater in number than their masters, the sea over full of fish would swell, and the neglected diamonds would so embellish the surface of the deep and stud it with their starry light that the inhabitants of the waters would grow used to a brilliant light and look even upon the sun without being affected by its brilliance.

Lines 760 and 761. I object very much to Vice being allowed to give rise to specious arguments while Virtue listens in silence without attempting to combat these.

Lines 992-998. Iris there with her rainbow waters the perfumed banks which caused the blossoming of flowers more mingled in colour than the edges of her embroidered scarf — (now listen mortals if your minds are pure enough to understand the real meaning of what I am going to tell you), and she drenches with dew from the fields of Elysium the beds of hyacinth and roses on which Adonis rests.

MILTON'S STYLE AND DICTION

We think of difficult phraseology when we first consider Milton's style, but it is well to realise that though this frequently occurs, the foundation of his work is a succession of plain familiar words in their natural order. Such sentences as

> Virtue could see to do what Virtue would
> By her own radiant light

(Lines 373 and 374)

occur very often, and the observation of these will rectify to some extent the general impression of the difficulty of the poet's language. Still it is obvious that very many sentences have a construction which appears singularly tangled. To Milton, of course, they were quite clear; he was so used to writing in Latin that an arrangement of words which is alien to English seemed to him the fit and proper mode of expressing his thoughts. Consequently we have (i) Latin constructions of *absolute clauses, e.g.*

> After the Tuscan mariners transformed,
> Coasting the Tyrrhene shore

(Lines 48 and 49)

and (ii) Greek idiomatic constructions such as that of putting a noun between two qualifying words, *e.g.*

> beckoning shadows dire

(Line 207)

as well as (iii) frequent inversions:

> Or straggling wether the pen flock forsook

(Line 499)

(iv) archaic phrases:

> I do not think my sister so to seek

(Line 366)

(v) the placing of adjectives after nouns:

>   No savage fierce
>
>   (Line 426)

(vi) compound epithets:

>   Either someone like us night-foundered here
>
>   (Line 484)

(vii) the Ethic Dative:

>   But of divine effect he culled me out
>
>   (Line 630)

(viii) condensed language:

>   Into swift flight till I had found you here
>
>   (Line 579)

and (ix) Ellipsis:

>   How chance she is not in your company?
>
>   (Line 508)

He uses many figures of speech, e.g. (i) *Metonomy* where a part i made to represent a whole:

>   Under the sooty flag of Acheron
>
>   (Line 604)

(ii) *Personification:*

>   And holy dictate of spare Temperance
>
>   (Line 767)

(iii) *Zeugma:*

>   Speaks thunder and the chains of Erebus
>
>   (Line 804)

where the verb *speaks* refers to something closely connected with it meaning and something else only remotely connected with it

(iv) *Metaphor:*

>   Unmoulding reason's mintage
>   Charactered in the face
>
>   (Lines 529 and 530)

(v) Exaggeration or *Hyperbole:*

>   Thrysis? whose artful strains have oft delayed
>   The huddling brook to hear his madrigal,
>   And sweetened every musk-rose of the dale?
>
>   (Lines 494-496)

(vi) Apostrophe:

>   O' thievish night
>
>   (Line 195)

(vii) Hypallage:

>   Or sound of pastoral reed with oaten stops
>
>   (Line 345)

where the epithet *oaten* belongs properly to the *reed* and not to the *stops*.

(viii) Simile:

> like a quivered nymph with arrows keen
>
> (Line 422)

and (ix) Alliteration:

> Dim darkness and this leafy labyrinth
>
> (Line 278)

It is noticeable that Milton generally uses *his* or *her* where we should normally employ *its*:

> Did a sable cloud
> Turn forth her silver lining on the night?
>
> (Line 222)

> Now the spell has lost his hold
>
> (Line 919)

The actual words he uses throw light upon his own vocabulary and on that of his age. We find many archaic words — innumerous (Line 349), swinked (Line 293), wain (Line 190), methought (Line 171), spets (Line 132), drouth (Line 66), and many words of Latin or Greek origin which seem pedantic now but were commonly used in the seventeenth century: votarist (Line 189), fantasies (Line 205), antiquity (Line 439), immured (Line 521). Milton loved a long list of names and in Lines 868 to 880 we have the splendid collection of *Tethys, Triton, Glaucus, Leucothea, Parthenope,* and so forth. To these he appends the permanent epithets *earth-shaking, hoary, tinsel-slippered* and thus vivifies each individual deity. He has adjectives which are unusual at times because they are compound, like *amber-dropping* (Line 863), at other times because of their spelling, like *azurn* and *turkis* (Lines 893 and 894).

Milton frequently has references to the Bible, *e.g.*

> his chamber in the East
>
> (Line 101) [Psalm xix, 5]

> the crown that virtue gives
>
> (Line 9) [Rev. iv, 4]

> the enthroned gods
>
> (Line 11) [II Timothy, iv. 8]

> that golden key
>
> (Line 13) [Matthew xvi, 19]

> pure-eyed Faith; white-handed Hope
>
> (Line 213) [I Cor. iii, 13]

and his language often seems scriptural in character. Sometimes Milton almost startles us with an Elizabethan feeling for Nature:

> Brisk as the April buds in primrose-season
>
> (Line 671)

but usually he uses Nature as the classical writers did in connection with the actions of the gods, thus giving a mythical representation of natural phenomena:

> There is a gentle nymph not far from hence,
> That with moist curb sways the smooth Severn stream

(Lines 824 and 825)

and his colours are sometimes more imaginative than natural; the bed of the Severn is hardly of the colour of coral — *thy coral-paven bed* (Line 886). On the other hand the *amber-dropping hair* (Line 863) is quite applicable to the river in spate, and *turkis-blue* and *emerald green* are colours that are sometimes seen in water. The use of Nature in connection with the pathetic fallacy must be noted too; the reference to *the kind hospitable woods* (Line 187) gives a vivid picture of the Lady's first idea of the woods.

The poet's likeness to Greek style is found not only in words and phrases but in the form of this work. In Lines 277 to 290 we have an example of Stichomythia, that is a form of writing in which question and answer are carried on in single lines:

> COMUS: Imports their loss beside the present need

(Line 287)

> LADY: No less than if I should my brothers lose.

(Line 288)

In order to appreciate the Miltonic power in the use of words and the phrasing of ideas it is necessary that *Comus* should be read aloud. Passages which appeal to the reader should be memorised, for fresh beauties are found during the repetition of lines. The following are merely suggestions for passages which might, with advantage, be memorised:

(i) The Songs in the Masque.

(ii) The Elder Brother's speech beginning:
> Peace, brother; be not over-exquisite
> To cast the fashion of uncertain evils:

(Line 359, *seq.*)

(iii) The Elder Brother's speech beginning:
> Yes, and keep it still

(Line 584, *seq.*)

(iv) The speech of Comus, beginning:
> I know each lane and every alley green

(Line 311, *seq.*)

THE DRAMATIC VALUE OF "COMUS"

Among his many ambitions Milton had a great desire to write a drama but his only two attempts were *Comus* and *Samson Agonistes*, and nearly forty years intervened between these experiments.

As a drama *Comus* is open to a certain amount of criticism, for the speeches are certainly rather long, though not longer than in many Shakespearian and modern plays, the action is improbable, the lesson is too openly shown, and the characters not sufficiently well-drawn.

Still it has some dramatic force and shares many qualities with the Greek drama. There is first a kind of Prologue formed by the speech of the Attendant Spirit (Lines 1-92). Then there appears a rout of monsters, and this, which really forms an Anti-masque, is connected with the dancing which was often incorporated in the Greek drama. After this, Comus appears and almost at the end of his speech more dancing takes place. The long speeches of Comus (Lines 93-169) and of the Lady (Lines 170-229) are quite in keeping with Greek dramatic tradition, as is also the dialogue which is carried on between them, each speaking an alternate line (Lines 276-290). When the Lady follows the supposed Shepherd, the first Act may be considered to end (Line 330). The second Act takes place between the two brothers, joined later by the Attendant Spirit (Lines 331-658). In the third Act there is a change of scene and in a stately palace Comus and the Lady carry on a dialogue (Lines 659-813). The fourth Act shows the ranting of Comus by the Attendant Spirit and the brothers, and in this part of the masque we have, too, the appearance of a classical nymph and her attendants, almost a *deus ex machina* effect (Lines 814-957). More dancing occurs, first in the form of an anti-masque when the country dancers perform, and later in more graceful measures *without duck or nod,* and there is a very short fifth Act (Lines 958-975) where the Attendant Spirit presents the Lady and her two brothers to their Father and Mother. Then comes an Epilogue, also a feature of Greek drama, in which the Attendant Spirit sets forth the purpose and moral lesson of the masque.

The best way to know any play or masque is to act it; *Comus* is particularly suited for this treatment, not because of its intrinsic dramatic qualities, but because the lyrical beauty of the verse can be brought out by speech. If it can be acted in the open, as happened a few years ago at Ludlow Castle, so much the better, but even if it has to be done indoors it is not difficult to represent a wild wood, a palace and a pastoral scene. Two painted back-cloths are all that is needed with brown curtains for the wood, and green for the last scene, or, indeed, the whole can be planned with curtains alone with a few cardboard trees to suggest a clearing in the forest. The scene in the palace can, of course, be entirely played with the help of curtains alone. When back-cloths *are* used, the scenes represented need only be suggestive: it goes without saying that Ludlow Town and the President's Castle would not be shown.

Ordinary garments of the Cavalier period will be used; the Attendant Spirit will need a shining multi-coloured garment at the beginning and end of the masque, and a shepherd's smock when in his disguise as Thyrsis. Comus must be beautifully dressed in a cloak which covers his shepherd's garb; this cloak will be doffed when he encounters the Lady and is mistaken by her for a *gentle shepherd,* and put on again in his palace. The followers of Comus are supposed to have *glistering apparel;* shining cloaks will serve the purpose, and the players should wear animal masks. Sabrina's costume and also that of the water-nymphs should be of soft clinging green material; and the dancers will wear the ordinary country dress as shepherds and shepherdesses.

THE CHARACTERS IN THE MASQUE
THE ATTENDANT SPIRIT

From the lips of this character proceed many of the author's own ideas on Virtue. He quotes freely from the Bible and from classical lore, pays a graceful compliment to the Earl and his family (Lines 30-35) and is in turn complimented (in his guise as Thyrsis, the shepherd) by the Elder Brother (Lines 494-496), is given the epithet *good* (Line 512), and shows his love for his supposed master's children — *my loved master's heir and his next joy* (Line 501), *your dear sister* (Line 564). In his spiritual state he has supernatural knowledge; he knows the right herb to use — *he called it haemony* (Line 638) — and the correct technique to employ:

> Without his rod reversed
> And backward mutters of dissevering power,
> We cannot free the lady that sits here
> In stony fetters fixed and motionless

(Lines 816-819)

and he can summon Sabrina when the other methods of undoing charms have not quite fulfilled their purpose:

> Some other means I have which may be used

(Line 821)

It is fitting that he who is the instrument in steering the story to its successful ending should be the Speaker of both the Prologue and the

Epilogue, and after presenting the children to their parents should voice the inner meaning of the whole masque:

> Love Virtue; she alone is free;
> She can teach you how to climb
> Higher than the sphery chime;
> Or if Virtue feeble were,
> Heaven itself would stoop to her.

(Lines 1019-1023)

[Henry Lawes, who, in the original production, took the part of the Attendant Spirit or Thyrsis, was in his boyhood a chorister, the son of a choirmaster at Salisbury Cathedral. He became a very good musician and was one of the Court musicians during the reign of Charles I. For part of his life he was a private music-master, and it was while he was acting in this capacity to the Earl of Bridgewater's children, that he composed the music for *Comus,* and was, in fact, instrumental in obtaining his friend Milton's consent to write the masque. After the death of Charles I he was reduced to comparative poverty, but at the accession of Charles II he gained favour at Court again and was the composer of the Coronation Anthem.]

THE LADY

The Attendant Spirit shows that *Comus* is based on the idea of virtue; the Lady embodies this quality in herself. Her character is only slightly drawn but it is not vague. She does not blame her brothers for leaving her on a very stupid excuse, but explains that they had gone:

> to the next thicket-side
> To bring me berries.

(Lines 185 and 186)

She makes no attempt at bravado but confesses she is frightened:

> a thousand fantasies
> Begin to throng into my memory.

(Lines 205 and 206)

However, she holds fast to Faith, Hope and Chastity, and believes that no harm can come to her, for, if necessary, an angel will come to her assistance. She is optimistic and ready to take heart again at the *silver lining* (Line 222). It would be unladylike to shout to her brothers, but she raises her voice in a song that illustrates her classical learning and her sisterly love for the

> gentle pair
> That likest thy Narcissus are.

(Lines 236-237)

In her conversation with Comus she is quite capable of carrying on a logical argument, and illustrates her point:

> Thou canst not touch the freedom of my mind
> With all thy charms.

She is not for a moment tempted in any real sense of the term. She will not yield to Comus because there is nothing in her character that will allow her to do so. She has no foes within the gate to take his part so the sophistry of this enchanter does not move her. Her words are noble, and Comus himself is moved by them:

> She fables not; I feel that I do fear
> Her words set off by some superior power.
>
> (Lines 800 and 801)

[The Lady was the Lady Alice Egerton, daughter of the Earl of Bridgewater, and in 1634 was between fourteen and fifteen years of age. She had had previous experience in acting as she had appeared in the short masque of *Arcades,* in which the words were composed by Milton and the music by Lawes.]

THE ELDER BROTHER

Probably the elder brother is an adaptation of Milton himself. He gives a wonderful picture of Virtue; his speeches are full of extra-ordinary purity and joy. At the first reading such speeches give the impression of much moralising and insufficient regard for the immediate danger of his sister, but the actor taking this part can bring out the feeling of consternation by varying his tone in the parenthesis — *as I trust she is not* (Line 370). It is difficult for him really to visualise any danger in which virtue can stand, because he is so certain of the *radiant light* which this quality bestows on those who possess it. His optimism is not without foundation; it is a part of his temperament:

> My nature is
> That I incline to hope, rather than fear
>
> (Lines 411 and 412)

but it is based also on the strength of Heaven and on that of Chastity. He is learned in classical lore and draws his examples of virtue equally from that and from Holy Writ.

He is not so lost in philosophy as to fail to be alert, however; he is as swift as his brother to hear *some far-off hallow break the silent air* (Line 481), and quite ready to meet any intruder with *iron stakes* (Line 491). When he hears that his sister is in the clutches of Comus he is full of ardent fire and decides that he will

> find him out
> And force him to restore his purchase back,
> Or drag him by the curls to a foul death
> Cursed as his life
>
> (Lines 606-609)

and he boldly attacks the deceiver and his rout.

[The Elder Brother's part was taken by John, Viscount Brackley, aged twelve, the eldest son of the Earl of Bridgewater. He had acted before in *Arcades* and also in Carew's masque *Coelum Britannicum,* for which Lawes had composed the music and in which Charles I had taken a part.]

THE SECOND BROTHER

This character is not as optimistic as his brother; his thoughts wander to all the dangers that may beset the lost sister. Like his brother he has a lyrical fluency in language, and he dwells on the beauty of Nature:

> The folded flocks penned in their wattled cotes
> Or sound of pastoral reed with oaten stops.
>
> (Lines 344 and 345)

He listens to his brother's remarks without sign of boredom in spite of his anxiety, and states that *divine philosophy* is

> musical as is Apollo's lute
> And a perpetual feast of nectared sweets.
>
> (Lines 477 and 478)

The last words we hear from him are a reproach to his brother:

> Is this the confidence
> You gave me, brother?

but he is not lacking in courage, and helps with drawn sword to overcome Comus. — *The brothers rush in with swords drawn, wrest his glass out of his hand and break it against the ground.*

[Like his brother, Mr. Thomas Egerton, aged ten, had already had some practice in acting, as he had taken a part also in Carew's *Coelum Britannicum.*]

COMUS

This being who represents many vices — intemperance, gluttony, rowdiness — is nevertheless made very attractive. He has ease and grace; he sings, he dances, he speaks with great eloquence. His lyrical strain is the most beautiful in the masque; it is he who describes the nocturnal dancers:

> The sounds and seas with all their finny drove,
> Now to the moon in wavering morrice move;
> And on the tawny sands and shelves
> Trip the pert fairies and the dapper elves.
> By dimpled brook and fountain-brim,
> The wood-nymphs decked with daisies trim,
> Their merry wakes and pastimes keep.

(Lines 115-121)

He draws his comparisons from Nature:

> Brisk as the April buds in primrose-season

(Line 671)

and talks of her

> full and unwithdrawing hand

(Line 711)

Like all the other characters in the Masque he is learned and can discourse on Stoics and Cynics, Jove-born Helena and Saturn, and there is a lulling cadence in the phrase:

> Refreshment after toil, ease after pain

(Line 687)

which is indicative of a poetic mind.

[The parts of Comus, his followers, the country dancers and Sabrina would be taken by professional actors.]

MILTON'S POETIC POWER

In *The English Muse* we are told by Oliver Elton that the verse of *Comus* goes *like a yacht before the wind,* and in poetic power Milton has certainly very few rivals. Sir Henry Wotton in his letter to Milton, written in connection with *Comus* speaks of a *Doric delicacy in your songs and odes,* and it is true that the harmony of the blank verse is reminiscent of Greek lyrical poetry. The beauty of Spenser and Fletcher and the Elizabethan lyrists seems to throb in Milton's lines, but above and beyond these reminiscences rings his own singing note. His power does not lie only in beauty of simple lines, though these are found too, but he has long passages, in which the musical theme seems to be caught up by each line from the last, to end in a climax of sound, which reverberates and re-echoes long after the actual words have died away. The poet's love of music is closely connected with his poetry in *Comus*. In his boyhood he sang madrigals in the fashion of his Elizabethan ancestors; he was accustomed to hearing lutanists, and probably played upon an instrument himself; his father was an accomplished musician, and his great friend, Henry Lawes, was responsible for the music at Court. It is no wonder then that music runs like a golden thread through the whole of *Comus,* gathering itself up at intervals into such sustained moments of lyrical beauty as can be found in the songs — *Sweet Echo; Sabrina fair; By the rushy-fringed bank; Back, shepherds, back; Noble Lord and Lady bright.* Lawes set these to music but they sing in the heart of the reader without any musical accompaniment. The first of these songs has lines of varying length, some being composed of only two feet, others of six. The rhyming lines are few but the absence of rhyme is not noticed, because the whole effect is so smooth and several of the sounds are fairly alike e.g. *pair* and *are, vale* and *well.* The Alexandrine at the end serves as both a climax and an echo, and gives *resounding grace* to the harmony of the verse.

In "Sabrina fair" the variation in the length of the lines helps the music of the first verse, and further aid to this musical quality is given by such words as *translucent, amber-dropping.* In the second verse we have an example of Milton's love of a catalogue of proper names: —Oceanus, Neptune, Tethys, Leucothea, Parthenope; such names seem to linger in one's memory, having almost a magical effect; and the compound words *tinsel-slippered, coral-paven* add charm also.

Sabrina's song *By the rushy-fringed bank* has *näiveté* owing to the unusual adjectives *azurn* and *turkis* with their delicate antique suggestion and the whole effect of the *rushy-fringed bank, the osier dank,* and the *printless feet* is deliciously refreshing.

In the three songs already mentioned some of the lines rhyme in couplets but this rhyme scheme is not invariable; alternate and irregular rhyme is also found, *e.g.* in the first verse of *Sabrina fair* the rhymes occur thus: — a b c b a d d c. In *Back, shepherds, back,* and *Noble Lord* and *Lady bright,* however, couplets occur throughout.

Couplets are found, too, in various parts of the masque though the main type of poetry employed is blank verse, that is, verse composed of iambic pentameters. Such couplets have mainly eight syllables in each line; in the speech of Comus (beginning at Line 93) this has the effect of speeding up the action. The same effect is gained in the question and answer between the Elder Brother and the Attendant Spirit (Lines 494-512), where the musical suggestion of the couplet form too is intended as a compliment to the musician Thyrsis, an effect gained earlier in the masque (Lines 87 and 88) by the use of alliteration. Speed is gained by the couplet-form too at the end, and

this lightness is in keeping with the suggestion of the Attendant
Spirit's return to his usual airy abode.

> I can fly or I can run
> Quickly to the green earth's end,
> Where the bowed welkin slow doth bend;
> And from thence can soar as soon
> To the corners of the moon.

(Lines 1013-1017)

Milton's favourite metre was blank verse, and this is used with excellent effect in the greater part of *Comus*. If every line, however, were
just composed of ten syllables with the accent falling on the second
syllable there would be a danger of monotony; consequently variation
is introduced. Very often the poet does not allow the sense of a
passage to be complete at the end of a line but carries it on to the
next, *e.g.*

> Wherewith she tamed the brinded lioness
> And spotted mountain-pard, but set at naught
> The frivolous bolt of Cupid.

(Lines 443-445)

An extra syllable is frequently added to a line, *e.g.*

> Think what and be advised; you are but young | yet |

(Line 755)

where it is placed at the end, and:

> As you imag|ine|; she has a hidden strength

(Line 415)

where it occurs in the middle.

Sometimes when it appears, however, that there is an extra syllable
in the line, this is not really so because syllables are elided, *e.g.*:

> May sit | i' the cen|tre and | enjoy | bright day |

(Line 382)

where *i' the cen* represents only two syllables instead of three. Variation is gained also by the use of different types of feet:

> Harpies and Hydras, or all the monstrous forms

(Line 605)

where trochees take the place of iambs at the beginning of the line.
This mixture of different types of feet is seen even more commonly
in the couplets than in the blank verse, and by such variation the
pace is quickened or retarded.

NOTES

1. **Jove's Court:** In the *Aeneid* Jupiter is represented as living in a starry
   chamber (*sideream in sedem*).

2. **Those immortal shapes:** In Latin the pronoun *ille, illa, illud* refers to a particular person or thing that is well-known. Milton here means "those of whom you know."

3. **Insphered:** Within their own spheres. An obsolete word. We still speak, however, of a person's *sphere, i.e.* the plane of society or of intelligence in which he moves. Milton believed in the Ptolemic theory of the Universe in which the Earth was considered to be the centre, and other bodies or spheres were fixed at different distances from it, keeping it enclosed. Plato thought there were eight of such spheres, the outer one being composed of fixed stars. Ptolemy stated that there were ten, the outermost being the *Primum Mobile* or *first-moved* which surrounded all the others. The music of the spheres was supposed by Shakespeare, following the theory of Pythagorus, to be made by the planets as they moved, but Milton suggests in his poem *Arcades* that it was produced by the nine Muses, each of which inhabited one of the nine inner spheres.

7. **Pestered:** From French *empêtrer,* meaning "to shackle a horse while he is feeding in the pasture." (Latin *pastus* from *pascere,* to feed.)

7. **Pinfold:** A place of confinement for cattle. A *pound* in which stray cattle were placed until claimed by their owners (Anglo-Saxon: *pindan,* to enclose). In *Pickwick Papers,* by Dickens, there is a reference to Mr. Pickwick being placed in a pound when incapable of getting home, and in a provincial paper in 1877, the following reference occurs: "Impounded in the pinfold, Edward Street, Leeds, a brown mare. If not claimed before Tuesday next, will be sold. H. Wright, Pindar."

16. **Ambrosial:** Immortal. Ambrosia was the food of the gods, and was supposed to confer immortality on all who partook of it.

16. **Weeds:** Garments. Shakespeare speaks in *A Midsummer Night's Dream,* of a "weed wide enough to wrap a fairy in." The word is only used now in connection with *widow's weeds.*

20. **Took in by lot:** In the *Iliad* the story is told of how, after the three sons of Saturn (Neptune, Jupiter and Pluto) had over-thrown their father, they divided his kingdom by casting lots for it. High Jove or Jupiter gained the heavens, Neptune the sea, and Pluto or Jupiter Stygius, the nether regions or Hades. *Nether* means *under* as in *netherlip* and *Netherlands.*

26. **Tridents:** The trident, or three-pronged sceptre, is a sign of the rulers of the sea. Neptune's trident would be very large, but those of the tributary gods would be small. (Lat. *tri,* three; *dens,* tooth.)

27. **The isle:** Great Britain.

29. **Quarters:** Divides into different parts. There is a suggestion that this refers to a division into *four* parts, because there were seats of government at Edinburgh and London, and Lords President governing Wales and the North.

29. **Blue-haired:** Generally **green-haired** is the epithet used for the sea-gods, but Ovid, in his description of such gods, connects them with the colour of the sea, calling them *caerulei dii.*

30. **This tract that fronts the falling sun:** Wales.

31. **A noble peer:** The Earl of Bridgewater who took up his duties as administrator of Wales and the English Counties of Gloucester, Worcester, Hereford and Shropshire in 1634. Accounts of his life show that he was an excellent man in both public and private life.

33. **An old and haughy nation:** The Welsh who inhabited Britain for more than five centuries before the birth of Christ, and held their land proudly for very many years against their invaders.

34. **Nursed in princely lore:** The children were well brought up in accordance with their high position. Also they were accustomed to frequenting the Court, and they were actually connected with royalty since their mother was the great-grand-daughter of the Countess of Clifford, daughter of Mary, the sister of Henry VIII.

37. **Perplexed: Intricate, entangled.** (Lat. *plectere,* to twist.)

38. **Horror:** Shagginess. (Lat. *horrere,* to bristle.)

39. **Forlorn:** Lost. (A.S. *forleosan,* to lose. *For* in A.S. often has a perorative effect. e.g. *forbid.*)

45. **Old or modern bard:** A reference to the custom of bards chanting their stories in the halls of nobles.

45. **Hall or Bower:** The hall was usually the banqueting-room, the bower the private apartment of the ladies.

46. **Bacchus:** The god of wine.

48. **After the Tuscan mariners transformed:** The story is told by Ovid that Bacchus, while on a voyage, hired a vessel belonging to some Etruscan (Tuscan or Tyrrhenian) pirates, who decided to sell him as a slave, though they had given their word to take him from Icaria to Naxos. He changed the pirates into dolphins, with the exception of the pilot, and the mast and oars of the ship into serpents. Tyrrhenia, in Central Italy, was called Tuscia or Etruria by the Romans.

50. **On Circe's island fell:** This island, Aeaea, is described in Homer's *Odyssey.* It is off the coast of Latium, but it was Ulysses, not Bacchus, who was cast on the island. His companions drank from Circe's enchanted cup, and were transformed into swine. But Ulysses, having already partaken of a root which prevented his enchantment, was able to force Circe to allow his men to take on human shapes once more. Circe was the daughter of the sun, and an ocean nymph.

58. **Comus:** The son of Bacchus and Circe. The word means in Greek, *merrymaking or revelling,* and Comus signifies *the god of Revel.* The word *comedy* may be noted in this connection also. The name had been used by other writers; it occurs in Ben Jonson's *Pleasure reconciled to Virtue,* and in the works of Massinger and Dekker as well as in the *Agamemnon* of Aeschylus, but in none of these writings is it used with exactly the connotation given by Milton.

60. **Celtic and Iberian fields:** France and Spain, in both of which countries much wine is produced.

61. **Ominous:** Full of bad omens, dangerous.

65. **Orient:** Bright, sparkling. The brightness of the sun begins in the east.

66. **Drouth of Phœbus:** Phœbus is the god of the sun, and the sun's heat causes thirst.

67. **fond:** foolish. (A.S. *fonnen,* to behave foolishly.)

71. **ounce:** lynx.

72. **All other parts remaining as they were:** In the account given in the Odyssey of the transformation of the sailors of Ulysses, the whole of the body became beast-like, but in Milton's story only the face was changed. This was probably because the actors in Milton's masque would wear their ordinary clothes with the addition of animal masks.

83. **Iris' woof:** Iris is the goddess of the rainbow. The warp in ·a cloth is composed of the threads which run lengthwise, the woof of those which run crosswise. (A.S. *wefan,* to weave.)

84. **A swain:** Henry Lawes, who was music master to the children of the Earl of Bridgewater, took the part of the Attendant Spirit, first in beautifully-coloured robes, and then in the garb of a shepherd. The *soft pipe* and *smooth-dittied song* are complimentary references to his music. The pipe was the usual musical instrument of shepherds.

93. **The star that bids the shepherd fold:** Hesperus, the evening star.

95. **Gilded car:** The golden chariot of Phœbus or Apollo.

96. **His glowing axle doth allay:** The ancients believed that when the sun set in the Atlantic ocean a noise like that of the hissing of the sea could be heard.

97. **Steep Atlantic stream:** Deep Atlantic ocean. The ancients thought that the ocean was a great stream surrounding the earth.

98. **Slope sun:** When the sun is sinking below the horizon it seems to send up a sloping or slanting beam.

105. **Rosy twine:** Wreaths or garlands of roses.

110. **Grave saws:** Wise sayings, Shakespeare, in *As You Like It,* refers to "wise saws and modern instances."

112. **Starry quire:** An allusion to the music of the spheres. (See note on Line 3.)

115. **Sounds:** Straits. A.S. *sund* means "swimming," so a sound is something that can be swum across.

116. **To the moon:** Under the influence of the moon. The tides are affected by the moon.

116. **Wavering morrice:** The morrice or morris or moorish dance was brought into Spain by the Moors. Later John of Gaunt introduced it into England. Many characters took part in costume in these dances, and a hobby-horse was often used. The waves seemed as if they were rearing themselves up and blowing as in a morrice-dance.

121. **Wakes:** Originally a wake was a *watching* during the night before the burial of someone who had died. (A.S. *wacian,* to watch.) Then it came to mean the watching on an evening before any holy day or before such a festival as the dedication of a church. Later it gained the mean-

ing of any merrymaking which was carried on late at night. In Lancashire annual wakes are still held when the people living in certain towns go away for a holiday, and business is practically at a standstill.

129. **Cotytto:** A Thracian goddess, corresponding to the Syrian Ashtorath, who was connected with all forms of licentiousness. Her worshippers were called Baptae because they were *sprinkled* with warm water during the rites which were held at night, hence "dark-veiled."

132. **Spets:** Casts forth, spits.

132. **Stygian darkness:** The river Styx was in Hades, so *Stygian darkness* refers to the gloom of the underworld.

135. **Hecate:** A goddess of sorcery and witchcraft, a suitable companion for Cotytto. She is identified with Luna (goddess of the moon), Diana (goddess of hunting), and is sometimes given the name of Proserpina when regarded as the goddess of Hades. Shakespeare refers to her as the leader of the witches in *Macbeth,* and she was popularly supposed to haunt the abodes of the dead, and to send demons and ghosts to frighten the living.

139. **Indian Steep:** The Himalayas were thought to be the eastern boundary of the world.

140. **Cabined loop-hole:** Narrow opening. An allusion to the first streak of dawn. The Persians have a legend that the sun first peeps through a hole in one of their mountains before rising above the top of the mountain.

147. **Shrouds:** Places of hiding. (A.S. *scrud,* clothing or covering.) The word *shred* is connected with this. The shrouds near St. Paul's Cathedral, was the name given to a covered place where sermons used to be preached in wet weather.

147. **Brakes:** Thickets.

150. **Charms:** Spells. (Lat. *Carmen,* a song.) Sorcerers used to recite verses.

151. **Wily trains:** Guileful methods which will attract. (Lat. *trahere,* to draw.)

155. **Blear illusion:** Blinding deception. Something which deceives by blurring the vision.

161. **Glozing courtesy:** Flattering kindness. (Middle English *glose,* an explanation, hence our word *glossary.*)

174. **Loose unlettered hinds:** Rough, ignorant peasants.

176. **Pan:** the god of shepherds; he is generally represented as half a man and half a goat and as playing on a pipe, the instrument of his own invention.

178. **Swilled:** Drunken. (A.S. *swillian,* to wash, hence "to drink greedily.")

179. **Wassailers:** Revellers. Those who drink healths. (A.S. *waes hael,* be strong.)

189. **Votarist:** One who has made a vow. (Lat. *votum.*)

189. **Palmer's weeds:** A palmer is one who has made a pilgrimage to the Holy Land and carried a palm-branch to show this. His garment was usually composed of a grey cassock and hood.

190. **Phœbus' wain:** The car of day. (A.S. *wegan,* to carry.) The time represented is evening.

215. **Chastity:** It is *Charity* which is generally connected with *Faith* and *Hope,* but Milton wishes in this poem to lay particular stress on Purity.

222. **her:** Milton uses the feminine possessive adjective because *nubes,* the Latin word for *cloud,* is feminine.

230. **Echo:** This nymph was in love with Narcissus, a very beautiful youth who, however, was so interested in his own beauty that he could pay no attention to anyone. Echo, finding her love was not returned, pined away until nothing was left of her except her voice.

231. **Airy shell:** The atmosphere which hides Echo.

232. **Meander:** A river which rises in Phrygia, Asia Minor, and is remarkable for its winding course.

232. **Margent:** Margin.

234. **Love-lorn:** Deprived of her loved one. There is a Greek legend which describes how Aedon killed her own son by mistake, and mourned for him.

237. **Narcissus:** For falling in love with his own image Narcissus was punished by being changed into the flower that bears his name; the head of which always droops downward.

241. **Sweet Queen of Parley:** Echo seems to parley or carry on a conversation with the speaker. (Fr. *parler,* to speak.)

241. **Daughter of the Sphere:** She is regarded as being connected with the music of the spheres.

242. **Translated:** Removed without dying.

243. **Resounding grace:** The charm given by the repetition of an echo. Heaven's harmonies were too great to be heard by the ordinary human ear but might be heard when softened to an echo.

251. **The raven down:** Night is represented as a winged goddess with feathers as black as those of a raven.

253. **Circe with the Sirens Three:** The three Sirens were sea-nymphs called Ligea, Parthenope and Leucosea, who lived on a rocky island near Sicily and by their sweet singing inveigled sailors on to the rocks. They really had no connection with Circe, except that she too could lure men to destruction by her singing.

254. **Naiades:** River-nymphs. Nereides were sea-nymphs, Oreades, mountain-nymphs, and Dryades, wood-nymphs. The river-nymphs were supposed to have tunics decorated with flowers. Ovid represents them as gathering herbs and flowers.

257. **Lap it in Elysium:** Enfold it in happiness. Elysium was the paradise of the Greeks, where the happy souls went after death.

257. **Scylla:** A monster who lived near the south-west coast of Italy, on the mainland side of the Straits of Messina. She was supposed to be surrounded by barking dogs, or, according to some writers to bark like a dog herself.

259. **Charybdis:** A monster that dwelt on the opposite side of the Straits of Messina on the coast of Sicily. Thrice daily she sucked in the water in the Straits and threw it up again, that is, she was a whirlpool.

268. **Sylvan:** Sylvanus, a god of the woods. (Lat. *silva*, a wood).

290. **Hebe:** The goddess of youth. She was cup-bearer to the gods.

293. **Swinked:** *Tired.* (A.S. *swincan,* to work). Chaucer speaks of the plough-man as being "a trewe swynker."

301. **Plighted:** Interwoven or folded. The word is connected with *plait.*

312. **Dingle:** A narrow valley.

312. **Dell:** A valley, not necessarily very narrow..

312. **Bosky bourn:** A stream with bushes growing along its banks.

315. **Stray attendance:** Your attendants who have strayed.

340. **Long levelled rule:** The beam of light looks as straight as a carpenter's ruler.

341 and 342. **Stars of Arcady** and **Tyrian Cynosure:** These terms refer to those constellations or groups of stars known as the Great Bear and the Lesser Bear. The Great Bear was that by which the Greek sailors steered, and the Lesser Bear that by which the Phœnician sailors, whose chief town was Tyre, steered. The Lesser Bear was often called Cynosura, the Dog's Tail, because part of it resembled a dog's tail curled up. Milton uses the phrase "the cynosure of neighbouring eyes" in *L'Allegro.* Both constellations are connected with Arcady since Callisto, an Arca-dian nymph, the daughter of Lycaon, King of Arcadia, was changed by Zeus or Jupiter into the Great Bear, and her son Arcas was trans-formed into the Lesser Bear.

344. **Wattled cotes:** Sheepfolds made of twigs or stakes that are plaited or wattled. (A.S. *watel,* a hurdle).

345. **Pastoral reed with oaten stops:** It was popularly thought that the shepherds made their pipes from oat-stalks, and *oaten* was used later for whatever material was employed for these pipes. The stops are the holes over which the performer's fingers are placed, and *oaten,* of course, applies really to the whole pipe, and not to the stops. In *Hamlet* we have a reference (III. ii. 372) to these pipes and their vent-holes or stops.

359. **Over-exquisite:** Too curious, too inquisitive. The Latin *exquirere* is used in a literary sense to mean "to look closely into some matter."

366. **To seek:** An old phrase meaning "having to seek," therefore "in want of." Milton uses the phrase in *Paradise Lost,* Book VIII, Line 197, "un-practised, unprepared, and still to seek," and Bacon has it in his essay *Of Usury,* "The merchant will be to seek for money."

367. **Unprincipled in Virtue's book:** Ignorant of the main points of Virtue.

378. **Plumes her feathers:** A term taken from falconry, meaning to *trim* the feathers.

380. **All to-ruffled:** Most editions print the phrase in this manner, but some have "all-to ruffled," others "all too ruffled," and those in Milton's own time have "all to ruffled." In the majority of editions, then, the phrase suggests that the "to" belongs to the participle and intensifies it, meaning "very much ruffled." In "all-to-ruffled" the sense is "entirely ruffled," in "all too ruffled" the idea is that "to" and "too" have been confused. Milton would have found every variation of the phrase in his time, e.g. in *Judges* ix. 53 the sentence occurs "A certain woman

cast a piece of a millstone upon Abimelech's head and all-to brake his skull," and in Chaucer's *Knight's Tale* we can read "all is to-broken thilke religion (Line 2759), while Shakespeare declares that an argument is "all too heavy to admit of much talk" (2 Henry IV. v. 2).

382. **Centre:** The idea given is that the centre will be in darkness.

389. **Senate-house:** Milton may be thinking of the calm which is associated with a University Senate, or remembering that the Romans regarded the Senate House as a spot that was inviolable.

390. **The fair Hesperian tree:** One of the labours of Hercules was to steal the apples from this tree, having first killed the dragon, Ladon, which guarded it. The tree on which grew golden apples was presented by Ge, the Earth, to Hera or Juno, on her marriage with Zeus or Jupiter, and given into the keeping of the Hesperides, the daughters of Hesperus, the Evening Star.

395. **Unenchanted eye:** Before being killed, dragons generally had to be "enchanted" and sent to sleep. Jason was able, for example, to win the Golden Fleece because Medea put a "sleepless" dragon to sleep.

404. **It recks me not:** I do not heed. The verb is used impersonally.

422. **Like a quivered nymph:** Spenser's Belphœbe who personified Chastity, carried "at her back a bow and quiver (*Faerie Queene*, Book II. verse III).

426. **Bandite:** Outlaw; someone put under a *ban*, from Italian *bandito*.

426. **Mountaineer:** a highwayman. Very often freebooters or robbers lived in mountains.

430. **Unblenched:** fearless. To *blench* is connected with *blanch*, to grow pale, and with *blink,* to look aside, both connected with the emotion of fear.

434. **Blue meagre hag:** Bloodless and thin crone. A *hag* is a witch, and the word is probably connected with A.S. *haga,* a hedge, since witches lived under hedges.

434. **Unlaid ghost:** Wandering spirit. It was thought that ghosts wandered on the earth from the time of curfew, about 8 p.m. until the first cock crowed. Shakespeare has various references to this in *Hamlet, The Tempest, King Lear.* Ghosts were *laid* by being exorcised by priests.

436. **Swart faery of the mine:** In Scandinavian mythology, mines were supposed to be haunted by gnomes who guarded hidden treasure. They were called "swart" or "black" goblins.

441. **Huntress Dian:** Diana, the goddess of hunting, was also the goddess of chastity, being insensible to the darts of Cupid, the god of love. She is usually represented with a bow, quiver, and "silver-shafted" arrows.

443. **Brinded:** Brindled or streaked.

447, 448. **Snaky-headed Gorgon shield that wise Minerva wore:** The Gorgons were three female monsters whose hair was formed of snakes. Medusa, the chief of the three, was so fearful that whoever looked at her was immediately turned into stone. She was killed by Perseus who had been given a shield by Athene; he cut off the monster's head by looking not at her but at her image in the shield. Athene or Minerva, the goddess of wisdom, placed the head in the centre of her shield and was thus able to frighten her enemies and withstand the darts of Cupid.

460. **Cast a beam on the outward shape:** Make the body as glorious as the soul.

468. **Imbodies and imbrutes:** Makes material and brutish instead of spiritual.

471. **Charnel vaults:** Tombs. (Lat. *caro, carnis,* flesh.)

478. **Apollo's lute:** Apollo was the god of the sun, and of music. He is often represented as playing the lyre or lute. In Shakespeare's *Love's Labours Lost* the words occur "As bright Apollo's lute, strung with his hair" (IV. iii. 342).

480. **Crude surfeit:** Undigested over-abundance.

483. **Night-foundered:** Overwhelmed by darkness. To founder is to go to the bottom (Lat. *fundus,* bottom) so the meaning here is "to be completely lost."

494. **Thyrsis, whose artful strains:** Thyrsis is traditional name for a shepherd, and in Milton's elegy *Epitaphium Damonis* the poet applies it to himself. Here it is the name given to Lawes, and an implied compliment is paid to his music by the words "artful strains."

495. **Huddling brook:** The confined idea of the water hastening and crowding.

495. **Madrigal:** A kind of musical composition very common in Shakespearian times, and in the time of Milton. It was a rhymed pastoral poem set to music, introduced from Italy. (Italian *madrigale,* from *mandra,* a flock.) It was quite common at feasts for a number of these madrigals to be set before the guests who took pleasure in singing them at sight.

499. **pent:** enclosed. (See note on *pinfold,* Line 7. *Pent* and *pin* are closely connected.)

501. **next joy:** the Second Brother.

515. **Sage poets:** Homer and Virgil. Homer told the tale of the Chimera in speaking of the adventures of Bellerophon, and also mentioned the enchanted islands of Circe and Calypso; and Virgil told of the descent of Orpheus to Hell through the cleft or rifted rocks of Cape Taenarus, in south Greece. Later writers such as Tasso, Ariosto and Spenser dealt also with the same stories, but Milton almost certainly here refers to the classical writers.

517. **Chimeras:** The Chimera was a fire-breathing monster, with the body of a goat, the head of a lion, and the tail of a dragon. (Greek *chimaira,* goat.) It was killed by Bellerophon, who rode on the winged horse Pegasus. It was such an unnatural monster that we now use the word "chimerical" to denote anything which is connected with a wild freak of fancy.

520. **Navel:** *Centre.* The temple of Apollo in Delphi was spoken of as "the navel of the earth," and Shakespeare speaks of "the navel of the state" (*Coriolanus,* III. i. 123).

522. **Bacchus and Circe:** (See notes on Lines 46 and 50).

526. **Murmurs:** Incantations or spells.

529. **Unmoulding reason's mintage:** Destroying the signs of intellect which are stamped or "charactered" on the face. (*Mintage* comes from A.S. *mynet,* a coin).

535. **Hecate:** (See note on Line 135).

542. **Knot-grass:** Grass with a jointed stem.

553. **Drowsy-frighted steeds:** The horses of night are supposed to have been kept awake by the noise in spite of their natural drowsiness.

554. **The litter of close-curtained sleep:** Sleep is represented as being drawn in a closely-curtained chariot.

561, 562. **Create a soul under the ribs of Death:** Breathe life even into the dead. It has been suggested that the idea is taken from a picture in Quarles' *Emblems* where a soul in the figure of an infant is represented within the ribs of a skeleton, to illustrate the text, "Who shall deliver me from the body of this death?" (Romans, vii. 24).

581. **Triple knot:** The union of Night and Shades and Hell.

595. **Scum:** The refuse which collects on the surface of liquids. To *skim* is to take off the *scum*.

598. **The pillared firmament:** The firmament is regarded as the roof of the universe. The pillars are possibly the mountains. (Latin *firmus*, solid.)

602, 603. **Girt with all the grisly legions:** Surrounded by horrible myriads of followers.

604. **Sooty flag of Acheron:** Acheron was one of the four rivers of Hell. Here it is used for Hell itself. *Sooty* is *black*.

605. **Harpies:** Monsters, who had the heads of maidens, long claws and wings. They were known as "snatchers" because they tormented a blind soothsayer named Phineus by snatching his food away from him. Their faces are represented as being haggard, for they are continually in need of food.

605. **Hydra:** A monster with nine heads that lived in the marshes of Lerna. Whenever one head was cut off, two fresh ones grew in its place. It was slain by Hercules who cut off the heads and applied a burning iron to the wounds before any fresh ones had time to be grown. The word here refers to water-snakes in general.

607. **His purchase:** What he has stolen or acquired. (French *pouchasser*, to get by hunting.)

610. **Emprise:** Enterprise.

610. **Yet:** This is an elliptical form of speech. It means "in spite of the fact that it is useless."

619. **A certain shepherd-lad.** This refers to his friend Charles Diodati who was studying medicine at Cambridge while Milton was there. When Diodati died Milton wrote an elegy called *Epitaphium Damonis* (see note on Line 484) in which he refers to his friend's knowledge of herbs, and his love of imparting botanical facts.

627. **Simples:** Herbs which have a medicinal effect. They were composed of only *one* ingredient.

635. **Clouted shoon:** Coarse shoes which were very often patched. A "clout" is a "patch" and it is also a piece of iron fastened on to the shoes worn by peasants, somewhat in the style of the irons fastened to the clogs worn in Lancashire and some other parts of England. The first meaning is seen in the Anglo-Saxon word *clut*, meaning a patch, and the second is obvious in the following quotation from Shakespeare's *Cymbeline:*

> I thought he slept, and put
> My clouted brogues from off my feet, whose rudeness
> Answered my steps too loud.
>
> (IV. ii. 214-216)

636. **Moly:** This was the drink that Ulysses took to guard against the enchantments of Circe (see note on Line 50). In the *Odyssey* the drink is taken from the flower of a plant that is black at the root. It was given to Ulysses by Hermes (or Mercury).

638. **Haemony:** The name is invented by Milton. Haemonia was the old name of Thessaly which was regarded by the Greeks as a land of magic.

640. **Mildew blast:** A wind that causes plants to suffer from the blight known as mildew, which covers leaves with a sticky substance (A.S. *meledeaw*, honeydew.) The east wind was supposed to have this effect, and plants suffering from mildew infected others near them. Shakespeare makes Hamlet describe his uncle as being

> Like a mildewed ear
> Blasting his wholesome brother.
>
> (*Hamlet,* III. iv. 64 and 65)

642. **I pursed it up:** I took care of it in my wallet.

646. **Lime-twigs:** Birdlime used to be spread on twigs as a snare to catch birds.

651. **Break his glass:** In Spenser's *Faerie Queene* Sir Guyon breaks the cup of the Enchantress Excess as she is handing it to him:

> Who taking it out of her tender hand
> The cup to ground did violently cast.
>
> (II. xii., Lines 58 and 59)

653. **Seize his wand:** This seems a reminiscence of the scene in the *Tempest* where Caliban advises Trinculo and Stephano to burn Prospero's books, since the master's magical power lies in them.

> Burn but his books.
>
> (III. ii. 103)

655. **Like the sons of Vulcan vomit smoke:** Virgil states that one son, Cacus, vomited smoke when pursued by Hercules. Vulcan was the god of Fire.

660. **Alabaster:** A kind of marble, named from Alabraston, in Egypt.

661, 662. **As Daphne was, Root-bound, that fled Apollo:** Daphne, a daughter of the river-god Peneus was loved by Apollo who pursued her, but she asked Jove to protect her, and she was changed into a laurel-bush.

672. **Julep:** A drink. (Persian *julap*, rose-water.)

674. **Syrup:** A drink. (Arabic *sharab*, wine, from *shariba*, he drank.)

675. **Nepenthes:** Pain-dispelling. (Greek *ne*, not *penthos*, grief.)

675, 676. **The wife of Thone, In Egypt gave to Jove-born Helena:** Polydamna, the wife of Thone, an Egyptian, gave Helen of Troy an opiate which would dispel all grief and pain, and in order to make her husband Menelaus and his friends merry, Helen placed this drug in their wine.

700. **liquorish baits (lickerish baits):** Foods that tempt the appetite; something that makes one "lick one's lips."

707. **Those budge doctors of the Stoic fur:** The word *budge* means "lambskin fur," *i.e.* lambskin with the wool worn on the outside as happens

in the decoration of the hoods of bachelors of Arts in certain Universities. It seems curious to use the word in this sense, however, when it is followed by "fur," and it seems likely that in Milton's day "budge" signified "stiff" or "surly." Milton's friend, Thomas Elwood, certainly used it thus when talking of a certain warden as a "budge old fellow." Here "fur" is used to denote a scholastic or professional sect, just as "ermine" denotes a judge, or "the cloth" is used as a generic term for clergymen. The meaning then is "Those solemn doctors who belong to that philosophical sect known as Stoics." The Stoics were founded in the third century B.C. by Zeno, who held his school under a porch at Athens, and they affected to take no notice of either pleasure or pain. (Greek *stoa*, a porch.)

708. **Cynic tub:** The Cynics were philosophers founded by Antisthenes in the fifth century B.C. at Athens. They despised pleasure and all forms of comfort, and one of their leaders, Diogenes, even lived in a tub. Their name is connected with the dislike shown by a dog for conventional society. (Greek *kyon*, a dog.)

719. **Hutched:** stored up. (French *huche*, a chest.)

721. **pulse:** Dried peas. Daniel and his companions fed on pulse (Daniel i. xii.)

734. **They below:** The denizens of the deep, who would find the sunlight no stronger than that given out by the diamonds that had not been mined.

745. **Nature's brag:** The thing of which Nature boasts.

750. **Sorry grain:** Poor colour. (Lat. *granum*, an insect, referring especially to the cochineal insect which gives a dark red dye.)

752. **vermeil-tinctured:** Red. (Lat. *vermis*, a worm; probably in reference to Cochineal insect.)

760. **Bolt her arguments:** Sift or pick out her reasons. Part of the machinery of a flour-mill is called the "boulting-mill" and this separates the flour from the bran. The word is found in various other writers, *e.g.* in Chaucer:

> But one cannot boult it to the bran.
> (*Nun's Priest's Tale,* Line 474)

in Spenser:
> Saying he now had boulted all the flour.
> (*Faerie Queene,* II. iv. 24)

and in Shakespeare:
> He has been bred in the wars
> Since he could draw a sword, and is ill-schooled
> In *boulted* language; meal and bran together
> He throws without distinction.
> (*Coriolanus,* III. i. 322)

790. **Dear wit:** Cleverness which is precious to *you.*

790. **Gay rhetoric:** Showy skill in speech.

791. **Dazzling fence:** Plausible methods of disputing. The idea is taken from the art of fencing. We still speak of "fencing with a question."

803, 804. **The wrath of Jove speaks thunder and the chains of Erebus:** The allusion is to be the ten years' war waged by Jupiter against his father

Saturn and the Titans. He used thunderbolts to overcome them and finally imprisoned them in Erebus, the lowest region of Hades.

808. **Canon laws:** Ecclesiastical rules. Comus speaks of his rabble as if it were a religious order.

809. **Lees:** Dregs.

810. **Settlings of a melancholy blood:** The Ancients believed that the body was composed of four *humours* — blood, phlegm, choler and melancholy — and a person's temperament was dependent upon the ascendancy of one or another of these. The melancholy humour was considered likely to lead to mental disorder, if it appeared in excess:

Nash in *Terrors of the Night* (1594) declares — "melancholy sinketh down to the bottom like the lees of the wine, corrupteth the blood and is the cause of lunacy."

816. **Without his rod reversed:** According to Ovid the wand of Circe was passed over the heads of the followers of Ulysses from left to right when the enchantress was ready to restore the men to their original forms. (*Metamorphoses*, XIV. 300.)

817. **Backward mutters:** The verses used as a charm had to be said backwards when disenchantment was to take place. This happens when Spenser describes how Amoret was saved by Britomart from the enchantment of Busirane. (*Faerie Queene*, III. xii. 36.)

822. **Meliboeus old:** This name occurs in one of the eclogues of Virgil, and is used as a traditional name for a shepherd. Here, however, some definite "shepherd" or "poet" is probably meant. It may be Geoffrey of Monmouth who wrote this story of Sabrina, but "soothest," meaning "most true," could hardly be applied to him as so many of his "chronicles" are "fables." Probably the reference is to Spenser who tells the story in the *Faerie Queene* (II. x. 14-19).

824 ff. **Sabrina:** In Milton's own *History of Britain,* the story of Sabrina is related. Here the author has altered it slightly in order to pay a prettier compliment to the Welsh people. The original story tells how Brutus built Troja Nova (the new Troy) which became London, and how, after his death, the kingdom was divided between his three sons, Locrine gaining the middle part, Loëgria, Camber taking Cambria or Wales, and Albanast ruling over Albania or Scotland. An enemy named Humber came against them; he was defeated and drowned in a river which since then has borne his name. Among the captives taken from Humber was Estrildis, a very beautiful maiden whom Locrine decided to marry. To do this he had to divorce his wife Gwendolen, who, terribly enraged, spent some years in Cornwall gathering an army together, and eventually was able to overcome Locrine and his followers. Locrine was killed by an arrow, and Gwendolen's revenge on Estrildis and her daughter Sabra or Sabrina, was to have them thrown into a river, and decree that the river should always be called Sabrina (afterwards changed to Severn) in memory of the wrong she had suffered from the child's parents.

828. **Brute:** Brutus was a mythical king of Britain. He was the grandson of Ascanius, who was the son of Aeneas and the grandson of Anchises.

835. **Aged Nereus:** A sea-god, the father of the Nereids or sea-nymphs.

836. **Lank head:** Drooping head.

838. **Nectared lavers:** Baths containing nectar, the drink of the gods. (Fr. *laver,* to wash.)

838. **Asphodel:** A flower which is a kind of lily which was supposed to grow in Elysium. Homer, in the *Odyssey,* makes his dead heroes recline in fields of Asphodel. Our word "daffodil" is connected with "asphodel."

839. **Porch:** Opening. Shakespeare uses the word in *Hamlet:*
> In the porches of mine ears.
>
> (I. v. 63)

840. **Ambrosial oils:** Ambrosia is the food of the gods; the oils, distilled from such food, would be very fragrant.

845. **Helping all urchin blasts:** Remedying all injuries caused by a hedgehog. The urchin or hedgehog was supposed, by country people, to do harm to cows; its ugliness and the fact that it was always seen alone increased their superstition concerning it. Mischievous spirits, too, were supposed sometimes to assume its shape. Shakespeare makes Caliban, in *The Tempest,* fear it:
> Fright me with urchin-shows.
>
> (II. ii. 5)

> Like hedgehogs, which
> Lie tumbling in my barefoot way, and mount
> Their pricks at my footfall.
>
> (II. ii. 10-12)

And it adds to the feeling of dire magic in *Macbeth:*
> *1st Witch:* Thrice the brinded cat hath mewed
> *2nd Witch:* Thrice. And once the hedge-pig whined.
>
> (IV. i. 1 and 2)

846. **Shrewd meddling elf:** Mischievous spirit. (A.S. *schrewen,* to curse.) Shakespeare refers to such elves, thus, in *Midsummer Night's Dream,* he calls Puck a "shrewd and knavish sprite" (II. i. 33), and in *King Lear* he attributes evil doings to "the foul fiend Flilbertgibbet" (III. iv. 108).

852. **The old swain:** Melibœus. (See note on Line 822.)

863. **Amber-dropping:** This is sometimes written without the hyphen where "amber" means "clear," and "dropping" means "falling." "Amber" can also be used as a synonym for "fragrant," as in *Samson Agonistes:* "an amber scent of odorous perfume," (Line 720). But anyone who has seen the Severn in spate will remember the yellow colour of the water, and will gain the idea of the bright golden hair of Sabrina hanging like a shower over her shoulders.

865. **Silver lake:** The Severn. "Lake" is sometimes used in classical writings to mean "river."

868. **Great Oceanus:** The most ancient god of the ocean, father of all the river-gods and the water-nymphs. He was supposed to surround the whole earth, hence the attribute "great" was generally applied to him in classical lore.

869. **Earth-shaking Neptune's mace:** The trident of Neptune, the god of the sea. "Earth-shaking" is the Homeric epithet applied to Neptune, just as "great" is to Oceanus.

870. **Tethys' grave majestic pace:** Tethys was the wife of Oceanus. She was regarded as being very stately, and the usual Homeric epithet applied to her was "venerable."

871. **Nereus:** (See note on Line 835.)

872. **Carpathian wizard's hook:** Virgil tells the story of Proteus who was Neptune's shepherd and therefore carried a hook or crook to look after the herds of seals. He was a sea-god who had a cave in Carpathus, an island in the Aegean Sea. He had the power of changing himself into different forms. If, however, he could be caught asleep on his rock, he could be forced to tell of future happenings, but usually he changed his form before such capture was effected. We still use the word "protean" to mean "changeable."

873. **Scaly Triton's winding shell:** Triton was the son of Neptune and Amphitrite, and was half a fish and half a man, therefore called "scaly" owing to his fish-like nature. At the command of Neptune he would blow his shell to soothe the waves. The shell would be "winding" because of its convolutions, or the word may be used in the sense of "winding a horn" as a hunter or herald does. Milton actually speaks of Triton as a herald in *Lycidas*:

> Now my oar proceeds
> And listens to the herald of the sea,
> That came in Neptune's plea.

> (Lines 88-90)

874. **Old soothsaying Glaucus' spell:** Glaucus was a fisherman who ate of a herb that had been sown by Saturn, and consequently gained the power of telling the future. Sailors believed in him and considered him as their special soothsayer or oracle. (A.S. *soo*, true.)

875. **Leucothea's lovely hands:** Leucothea or Ino, in order to escape the anger of her husband Athamas, who had become mad, threw herself into the sea, and was changed into a sea-deity, known as "the white goddess" from the whiteness of her skin.

876. **Her son that rules the strands:** Leucothea or Ino took with her Melicertes her son, and he too was changed into a sea-deity under the name Palæmon or Portumnus; he was made god of harbours.

877. **Thetis' tinsel-slippered feet:** The Homeric epithet applied to Thetis is "silver-footed." Thetis was a daughter of Nereus and the mother of Achilles.

878. **Sirens:** (See note on Line 253.)

879. **Dead Parthenope's dear tomb:** Parthenope was supposed to be buried at Naples; in the poetry of Vergil this town is sometimes called Parthenope.

880. **Fair Ligea's golden comb:** Ligea, another Siren, is here represented as combing her hair, like a mermaid.

893. **Azurn:** Azure.

894. **Turkis:** Turquoise. The turquoise was so-called because it came from Persia through Turkey.

921. **Amphitrite:** The wife of Neptune.

923. **Sprung of old Anchises' line:** Locrine was in the direct line of descent from Anchises (see note on Line 828).

929. **Thy tresses fair:** The leaves of the trees that grow on the banks of the Severn.

933. **Beryl:** A precious stone of a greenish yellow colour. It is sometimes used as a magic crystal in which the future is supposed to be visible. It is certainly not found in Wales, but Milton may have in mind some connection between its yellow colour and the waters of the river, and also some suggestion of a fortunate future.

933. **Golden ore:** Here again the suggestion of the yellow colour may have caused the use of the phrase. A certain amount of gold has, however, been found in the Welsh mountains, and some of this Welsh gold was used in the making of the Duchess of Kent's wedding-ring in 1934.

937. **Myrrh and Cinnamon:** Myrrh is aromatic gum, and cinnamon the spicy bark of a laurel. Neither are found in England, but Milton wants to give the idea of a sweetly-smelling grove.

963. **Mercury:** The Messenger of the gods and the patron of dancing. He had wings on his ankles so was very light-footed.

964. **Mincing Dryades:** Wood-nymphs taking small steps.

982. **Hesperus and his daughters three:** (see note on Line 393).

986. **The Graces:** The three Graces were especially known for their courtesy and delight in innocent enjoyments. Euphrosyne signified light-heartedness, Aglaia, brightness and Thalia, beauty.

986. **Rosy-bosomed Hours:** One of the Homeric epithets is used here; Homer also employs "rosy-fingered." The Hours were the goddesses of the seasons.

991. **Nard and Cassia:** Aromatic plants that grow in the East. Nard is Spikenard.

995. **Purfled:** with an embroidered edge. (Fr. *pourfiler,* to work on the edge.) The word is found in Spenser.

996. **Adonis:** When Adonis, a beautiful youth loved by Venus, was killed by a boar, Venus was so overcome with grief that the gods allowed him to spend six months of every year on earth with her. These months were spent in a beautiful garden, associated in this poem with the garden of the Hesperides.

1002. **The Assyrian queen:** Venus, who was worshipped by the Assyrians under the name of Astarte or Ashtaroth.

1004, 1005. **Celestial Cupid, her famed son, advanced, Holds his dear Psyche:** Venus was envious of the beauty of Psyche so ordered her son Cupid to inspire her with love for some contemptible man. He visited Psyche in order to carry out his mother's wishes but fell in love with her himself. He warned her not to try to find out who he was, but she, being overcome by curiosity, lit a lamp and looked at him while he was asleep. A drop of hot oil fell on him and he awoke and fled from her presence. Psyche wandered about looking for him, and at last reached the palace of Venus, who persecuted her and made her a slave. Cupid rescued her and by his help she became immortal, and the two were united. The myth of Cupid and Psyche represents the union of love and the human soul after the latter has been fitted for this heavenly union by being disciplined and purified on earth. The story is told by Spenser in the *Faerie Queene* (III. vi. 46 ff).

1015. **Bowed welkin** The sky formed like an arch.

1021. **The sphery chime:** The music of the spheres. The ancients thought that as the planets moved in their orbits around our earth, which they regarded as fixed, these produced musical sounds which formed a perfect harmony. In spite of his visit to Galileo, Milton still believed that the earth was the centre of the universe and that the other heavenly bodies moved around it.

1022. **If Virtue feeble were:** Milton wrote this and the succeeding line in an autograph book when passing through Geneva during his Continental visit.

QUESTIONS

1. How far does *Comus* conform to the requirements of a true masque?

2. Dr. Johnson's criticisms on *Comus* run as follows. How far are they true?

   (a) A work more truly poetical is rarely found; allusions, images and descriptive epithets embellish almost every period with lavish decoration. (N.B. — "period" means "sentence.")

   (b) As a drama it is deficient. The action is not probable.

3. Do you agree with Macaulay that "the piece must be regarded as a poem"?

4. Consider the anti-masques in *Comus*.

5. What remarks would you make about the following criticisms:

   (a) With Milton, each real person tends to become the representative of an idea or group, more or less complex, of ideas (Dowden).

   (b) *Comus* is a suite of speeches, not interesting by discrimination of character; not conveying a variety of incidents, nor gradually exciting curiosity; but perpetually attracting attention by sublime sentiment, by fanciful imagery of the richest vein, by an exuberance of picturesque description, political allusion and ornamental expression (Warton).

6. Dr. Johnson decided that *Comus* was "tediously instructive." Do you agree with this?

7. State the "order" in which the following lines appear:

   (i) Longer I durst not stay, but soon I guessed
   You were the two she meant

   (ii) Shepherd, 'tis my office best
   To help ensnared chastity.

(iii) And left your fair side all unguarded, lady?

(iv)   I'll hallo,
      If he be friendly, he come well.

(v) Noble lord and lady bright
      I have brought ye new delight.

(vi) Why are you vexed, lady? why do you frown?

(vii) Perhaps some cold bank is her bolster now.

(viii)   'Tis likeliest
      They had engaged their wandering steps too far.

(ix) Sweet queen of parley, daughter of the Sphere.

(x) She fables not. I feel that I do fear
      Her words set off by some superior power,

(Use the letter a to denote which speech comes *first* in the masque, b to denote which comes *second* and so on.)

8. Where in the masque is reference made to the following:

(a) A goddess whose robes are woven of many colours.

(b) A nightingale.

(c) Faith and Hope.

(d) Scylla and Charybdis.

(e) The early rising of the lark.

(f) The tree bearing the golden apples.

(g) The lute of Apollo.

9. Give an account of the origin of the Masque.

10. Show what Milton made of the "masque" form.

11. To what extent are Milton's own thoughts revealed in *Comus*.

12. Sir Henry Wotton wrote in a letter to Milton: "I should much commend the tragical part if the lyrical did not ravish me with a certain Dorique delicacy in your songs and odes, whereunto, I must plainly confess to you, I have seen yet nothing parallel in our language." By paying careful consideration to the tragic and the lyric parts of the work give your decision as to this being a just criticism.

13. Macaulay points out that Milton's masque is "essentially lyrical and dramatic only in semblance." By close examination of the lyrical elements, give a careful estimate of their qualities.

14. "The speeches must be read as majestic soliloquies; and he who so reads them will be enraptured with their eloquence, their sub-

limity, and their music" (Macaulay). By quotation from the speeches, discuss their eloquence, sublimity and music.

15. Do you consider that the long dialogues spoil the masque?

16. Is Wordsworth's appreciation of Milton:
     "Thou hadst a voice whose sound was like the sea."
     applicable to the great poet's work in *Comus*.

17. Write short accounts of the following episodes in *Comus*:
    (a) The meeting of Comus and the Lady.
    (b) The rescue of the Lady.

18. Write explanatory notes on the following:
    (a) Thou shalt be our star of Arcady (Line 341).
    (b) I pursed it up but little reckoning made (Line 642).
    (c)   When the wrath of Jove
        Speaks thunder, and the chains of Erebus,
        To some of Saturn's crew (Lines 803-805).
    (d) Under the sooty flag of Acheron (Line 604).
    (e) And the swinked hedger at his supper sat (Line 293).
    (f) After the Tuscan mariners transformed (Line 48).

19. Describe carefully what happened immediately after:
    (i) The Attendant Spirit invoked Sabrina.
    (ii) The brothers dashed the glass of Comus to the ground.
    (iii) The Attendant Spirit realised that a sudden silence had taken the place of riotous noise.
    (iv) The Second Brother had expressed his views on "divine philosophy."

20. What picture does Milton give us of (i) the forest, (ii) the abode of Comus.

21. Judging from your reading of *Comus* what do you consider the main characteristics of Milton's style.

22. Illustrate from this masque the classical knowledge of Milton.

23. Give examples to show Milton's skill in the use of figures of speech.

24. Show that Milton used epithets in a very clever fashion.

25. Discuss the beauty of Milton's verse.

26. Consider the Puritan element in *Comus*.

27. Show that a serious moral atmosphere pervades *Comus*.

28. Dr. Johnson says: "*Comus* exhibits Milton's power of description and his vigour of sentiment employed in the praise and defence of virtue." Show how far you consider this is true.

29. Dr. Johnson did not appreciate the songs in *Comus*. He says: "They are full of imagery but harsh in their diction, and not very musical in their numbers." Write a contradiction to this criticism.

30. What impressions of Milton have you gained by reading *Comus*.

31. Show how the lyrics are interwoven with the story in *Comus*.

32. Show how *Comus* illustrates Milton's attitude towards the social religious conditions of his time.

33. A few years ago *Comus* was acted at Ludlow Castle. If you had had charge of the arrangements how would you have represented it? Design the costumes as well as the setting.

34. Give the arguments by which Comus tries to lead the Lady from the path of virtue, and her replies to his arguments.

35. Under what conditions are the following names introduced into *Comus*: Hecate, Sabrina, Iris.

36. Comment upon *Comus* as a dramatic work.

37. Illustrate from *Comus* (i) Milton's love of music, (ii) use of archaic words.

38. What influences of Spenser can you detect in *Comus*?

39. Which passages in *Comus* appeal to you as examples of especially good lyric poetry?

40. A masque is sometimes described as a combination of mystery play and pageant. Does *Comus* fit in with this description?

41. Write a short essay on the idea of liberty depicted in *Comus*.

42. Give a short outline of the story of *Comus*.

43. Show that the words: "Love Virtue, she alone is free" give a clue to the whole meaning of *Comus*.

44. Quote five or six passages which illustrate Milton's love of Virtue.

45. Imagine that a friend is criticising *Comus*. Give his or her criticisms and your own defence of the work.

46. Do you think that Milton himself had any sympathy with the character of Comus? Give your reasons.

47. How far is *Comus* autobiographical.

48. Give examples from *Comus* of (i) Compound words, (ii) Alliteration, (iii) Personification, (iv) a line that has more than the usual number of syllables, (v) A Simile.

49. In what connection do we hear of (i) Minerva, (ii) Elysium, (iii) Diana, (iv) The April buds, (v) The Carpathian wizard?

50. Illustrate from *Comus* the debt of Milton to (i) Plato, (ii) Shakespeare.

51. "Tinsel-slippered" (Line 877) is a Homeric epithet. Give other epithets from *Comus* that are reminiscent of Homer.

52. "Sabrina is her name." Discuss Milton's use of proper names in *Comus*.

53. "Enjoy your dear wit and gay rhetoric" (Line 790). What does the Lady mean by this remark? Give examples of the "wit" and "rhetoric" that have been employed.

54. Give clearly the references throughout the masque to Virtue.

55. Trace closely the argument between the Lady and Comus.

56. Give in detail the views of the Elder Brother and the objections to these raised by the Second Brother.

57. What references has Milton to Nature in *Comus*?

58. In what connection do we hear of the following: (i) a nymph that lives in a shell; (ii) a foreign wonder; (iii) a shepherd's pipe; (iv) a chimera; (v) a bright golden flower.

59. What useful information was the Attendant Spirit able to give the brothers?

60. Milton pays some charming and subtle compliments in *Comus*. Give the references to these, and discuss their suitability.

61.   Upon a bank
              With ivy canopied.
What flower was mingled with the ivy? What other references are there to flowers — or to fruit — in *Comus*?

62.   My nature is
        That I incline to hope rather than fear.
        Show that this is a true representation of the character of the speaker.

63.   Show that in *Comus* both beauty and ugliness are well described.

64.   Consider (i) the views of the Elder Brother on evil, (ii) the views of Comus on beauty.

65.   What references are there in *Comus* to (i) a dark chair, (ii) a scout, (iii) a lantern, (iv) a candle, (v) a sheep?

ANSWERS TO QUESTIONS 7, 8, 49, 58, 65

7.   viii. a; ix. b; iii. c; vii. d; iv. e; i. f; vi. g; x. h; ii. i; v. j.

8.   a, Line 83, b, Line 235; c, Line 212; d, Lines 258-260; e, Line 318; f, Line 395; g, Line 475.

49.   (i) Line 448; (ii) Line 257; (iii) Line 441; (iv) Line 671; (v) Line 872.

58.   (i) Line 230; (ii) Line 265; (iii) Line 345; (iv) Line 517; (v) Line 633.

65.   (i) Line 134; (ii) Line 138; (iii) Line 197; (iv) Line 338; (v) Line 499.

DAUGHTER TO THAT GOOD EARL

Milton addresses Lady Margaret Lay, a friend of his, whom he hails here with respect and affection. She was a daughter of the Earl of Marlborough and the wife of Captain Hobson, another friend of Milton's. He sees in her the living memory of her father.

I DID BUT PROMPT THE AGE

Here is expressed Milton's profound dismay at the tyrannical temper of the new Presbyterian government. The government he had espoused was failing him. He was bitter also because it had neglected to accept his own ideas of public administration and procedure. He here turns against the government and he becomes more or less of an independent in political matters. He ended as an out and out individualist, belonging to no group or sect.

IL PENSEROSO

Il Penseroso is a work which shows Milton as a reflective student thinking about the serious matters of life. The word does not mean "melancholy" as is sometimes inferred, but is really connected with our word "pensive"; the man described has a tranquil and contemplative but not a brooding or anxious mind. It is possible that *Il Penseroso* was written before *L'Allegro;* certainly Milton seems to have a preference for the "thoughtful" man. The ending of each poem clinches this impression Milton has no doubt that Melancholy can give pleasure.

> These pleasures, Melancholy, give,
> And I with thee will choose to live.

But he is not quite so sure about Mirth.

> These delights if thou canst give,
> Mirth, with thee I mean to live.

There is much in common between this lyric and Fletcher's poem, No. 104, and it is possible that it owes some ideas also to Burton's *Anatomy of Melancholy.*

Among the chief points to notice in *Il Penseroso* are the fine meditative passages free from any suggestion of narrow Puritanism; the metrical charm of the varied metre, *e.g.* in l. 121, where the extra stressed syllable gives the suggestion of the length of the night; the verbal felicity that makes one feel the words used are the only possible ones, *e.g.* "pale" (121), "civil-suited" (122), "storied" (159); and the charming pictures in ll. 56-62, 65-70, 121-130, 139-146.

Morpheus: god of Sleep. ("Morphia" is derived from the name.)

Prince Memnon: a very handsome Ethiopian prince who was slain by Achilles.

L'ALLEGRO

This poem and *Il Penseroso* were written during the six years (1632-1638) during which Milton lived with his father at Horton in Buckinghamshire after leaving Cambridge.

L'Allegro is really connected with the Latin "alacer" from which our word "alacrity" comes. It gives an idea of briskness, of boyishness, of cheerfulness. The sounds throughout the poem are cheerful — the lark's song, the whispering winds, the bells in the hamlets, and the hum of human voices in cities. The details given are not supposed to chronicle the events of one particular day but to give a list of the pursuits a man such as *L'Allegro* may be supposed to have followed. The two poems *L'Allegro* and *Il Penseroso* do not really typify two different men, but the same man in two moods. *L'Allegro* seems to be Milton himself enjoying a holiday. (A contrast between the two poems is given later.)

Among the chief points to notice in *L'Allegro* are the pastoral conception of the poem (*e.g.* ll. 64-69, 81 to 90); the classical knowledge shown (10-20, 145-150, etc.); the telling epithets, *e.g.* "ebon shades" (9), "twisted eglantine" (48), "russet lawns and fallows gray," (71), "whispering winds" (117); the beautiful description of Nature, magnificent in ll. 60-1, fresh in ll. 69-79, where no mere catalogue is given but the scenes are made to live in the reader's imagination; the rhythm of the verse, where the iambic measure is varied by trochees sometimes for several lines at a time; and the youthful quality of joy that pervades almost every line.

Cerberus: the three-headed dog that guarded the entrance to Hades.

Stygian cave: a cave near the River Styx in Hades.

Cimmerian desert: a dark desert supposed to exist at the edge of the world.

Euphrosyne: the Greek goddess of Mirth.

Hebe: cup-bearer to the gods.

eglantine: probably the honeysuckle.

tells his tale: counts the number (of his sheep). Anglo-Saxon "tellan" = "to count." The word "tally" is connected with this.

Cynosure: a star which helped sailors to guide their ships, probably the Lesser Bear. Here it means the center of attraction.

Corydon and Thyrsis: names of shepherds.

Phyllis and Thestylis: names of shepherdesses.

Hymen: god of Marriage.

Lydian airs: soft, pleasing, melodious poems.

Orpheus: Orpheus was a very skilful musician and when his wife Eurydice died he followed her to Hades and played so beautifully to Pluto, the god of Hades, that Pluto allowed him to take his wife back to earth. One stipulation was made, however — that neither should look back until they had completely passed out from Hades. Orpheus, unfortunately, on seeing the light of day as he neared the entrance, looked back, and Eurydice was immediately snatched back into Hades.

GENERAL COMPARISON AND CONTRAST OF "L'ALLEGRO" AND "IL PENSEROSO"

Though there are decided points of contrast in the two poems it is easy to find many ways in which they are alike. In fact Dr. Johnson criticises them for being too much alike. He says, "I know not whether the characters are kept sufficiently apart. No mirth indeed can be found in his melancholy, but I am afraid I always meet some melancholy in his mirth." The poems certainly have the same setting — both begin in the country and are connected with the town. The actions seem to take place in parallel form in the poems, though *L'Allegro* deals mainly with the sights and sounds of the daylight, and *Il Penseroso* is concerned for the most part with twilight. *L'Allegro* praises comedy and pleasant songs, *Il Penseroso* tragedy and organ-music, but they both thus show their connection with the theatre and music. In both the beauties of Nature are described, and both give many "pictures"; in each poem simple delights are praised. The metrical basis of each poem is alike — a line of four iambic feet varied by the insertion of trochees and pauses. Both show Milton's wide vocabulary and skill in the choice of words. Really it is true to say that the two poems are complementary rather than contrasting.

DETAILED COMPARISON OF "L'ALLEGRO" AND "IL PENSEROSO"

L'ALLEGRO	IL PENSEROSO
Banishment of Melancholy, 1-10.	Banishment of Mirth, 1-10.
Welcome to Mirth and account of parentage, 11-24.	Welcome to Melancholy and account of parentage, 11-30.
Companions of Mirth, 25-40.	Companions of Melancholy, 31-55.
Pleasures of morning, 41-68.	Pleasures of evening, 56-84.
Pleasures of afternoon, 69-99.	Pleasures of night, 85-120.
Pleasures of evening, 110-16.	Pleasures of early morning, 121-30.
Pleasures of night, 117-34.	Pleasures of later morning, 131-50.
Effect of Music, 135-50.	Effect of Music, 151-74.
Desire for Mirth, 151-2.	Desire for Melancholy, 175-6.

LADY, THAT IN PRIME OF EARLIEST YOUTH
Milton assumes the role of an old friend consoling a young girl who has been reprimanded. Interesting for its biblical imagery, this sonnet is one of his least artistic or appealing.

LYCIDAS
Milton himself has explained what he means the scope of *Lycidas* to be in the following words, "In this Monody the author bewails a learned friend unfortunately drowned in his passage from Chester on

the Irish Seas, 1637. And by occasion foretells the ruin of our corrupted clergy then in their height." The poem is thus an eulogy and a condemnation. Edward King, the "learned friend," had been a fellow-student of Milton at Christ's College, Cambridge, and after gaining his degree had remained at the College as a tutor and "fellow." When he was twenty-five he was drowned while crossing to Ireland, and his Cambridge friends, deciding to publish a volume of commemorative poems, asked Milton to send a contribution. The result was *Lycidas*. It is a pastoral elegy, modelled on the pastorals of Theocritus and Virgil, but Milton does not preserve the elegiac strain throughout. He uses the poem to give his views about the abuses of his own time, especially about the corruption in the Church, and to give his own feeling about the enduring power of fame. His tenderness for his dead friend, however, is quite sincere, and his poem ends like most elegies, with a reference to the triumph of the dead scholar.

> There entertain him all the saints above
> In solemn troops and sweet societies,
> That sing and singing in their glory move
> And wipe the tears for ever from his eyes.

In the Introduction to the poem Milton explains that he has undertaken the work although he had not meant to write any poetry until he had fully prepared himself for such a task (ll. 1-4). He then invokes the help of the Muses (15-22) and, pretending that he and Lycidas were fellow-shepherds, states how close their friendship had been (23-36). He shows how deeply he feels his friend's loss (37-49) and grieves that neither the nymphs nor the Muse herself could preserve his friend's life (50-64). Turning from the pastoral convention he discusses the true nature of Fame (64-84). He then returns to the pastoral and points out that even Neptune had not been able to save Lycidas (85-102). The drowned man is mourned by Camus (the University of Cambridge) (103-107) and by St. Peter (the Church) (108-113). Then, still keeping to the pastoral idea, Milton enters on a diatribe against those shepherds of the Church who neglect their duty and points out that their sloth and selfishness will be punished (113-131). Nature is next asked to bring her flowers to strew the hearse of Lycidas (132-151), and the writer of the poem wonders where the dead body is really laid (152-164). Then follows the noble thought that Lycidas is not dead but has joined the heavenly company (165-185), and finally Milton makes a reference to the song he has just composed and to his own life (186-193).

Among the many excellences of *Lycidas* the following may be particularly noted:—

(1) The appropriate imagery, *e.g.* the references to himself as a gatherer of fruits picking unripe berries and gathering leaves that are not ready to fall, to Lycidas as a shepherd, and to the River Cam.

(2) The variation of stress in the verse and the consequent avoidance of monotony, *e.g.* the short fourth line seems indicative of his rashness in undertaking this great work, the broken line (56) suggests the disjointed nature of a dream, the last two lines give the impression of lively movement.

(3) The irregular rhyme-scheme, *e.g.* ll. 1, 13 and 15, have no corresponding rhymes, sometimes couplets are used, sometimes alternate rhymes, sometimes the rhyming sound is greatly delayed. This seems to give an impression of the sea under which Lycidas lies, with wavelets coming at irregular intervals.

(4) Infrequent alliteration which is always melodious, *e.g.* ll. 142, 143, and 144.

(5) Repetition which often leaves a feeling of pathos, *e.g.* ll. 8, 9, and 10.

(6) The vowel sounds, which often give a lingering effect of sorrow, *e.g.* ll. 41, 42, 43, 58, etc.

(7) The use of a pause, marked sometimes by a dash, sometimes by a question mark, sometimes by a semi-colon.

(8) The classical allusions — Amaryllis, Neptune, etc.

(9) The delight in Nature. Most of the illustrations taken from Nature are simple and well-known, and the flowers are given with a flash of detail — "the rathe primrose," "the tufted crow-toe," "the pansy freak'd with jet," etc. (142-145). The only plant that does not quite seem to fit in is the "gadding vine" (40). The criticism that all these flowers do not bloom at the same time is beside the point. The point is that all the seasons bring their offerings.

(10) A number of expressions, *e.g.* (a) "blind mouths" (119), in which two ideas are involved, since the clergy in their corrupt ways of life are spiritually blind and they are also great gluttons for the material wealth and pleasure of this world, (b) the "two-handed engine" (130), which may mean the two-edged sword carried by the divine figure seen by Saint John (Revelation i. 16) or else the axe which is laid at the root of the tree (St. Matthew iii. 10).

(11) The contrast between the beautiful music of the rest of the poem and the harsh sounds in the words applied to the clergy, *e.g.* "scrannel" (124).

(12) The use of climax. "Creep and intrude and climb into the fold" (115).

(13) The dramatic use of Apostrophe when the Angel is addressed (163).

(A portion of Ruskin's *Sesame and Lilies* should be read in connection with the appreciation of *Lycidas*.)

Satyr: in Greek mythology imaginary creatures, half goats, half men.

Fauns: in Roman mythology, the same as Satyrs.

Damoetas: name of a Greek shepherd, here used for a Cambridge don.

shaggy Mona: the isle of Anglesey, which is well-wooded.

Deva: the River Dee, called "wizard" because Merlin lived near it. It was supposed to have the power of prophesying good or evil for Wales by changing its course.

Hebrus: a river of Thrace.

Lesbian shore: Lesbos was an island in the Aegean Sea.

Amaryllis . . . Neaera: imaginary names of shepherdesses.

Blind Fury: Milton really means "blind Fate." There were three Fates — Clotho who spun the web of man's life, Lachesis who measured it, and Atropos who cut it.

Arethuse: Arethusa was a fountain in Sicily.

Mincius: Mincius (or Mincis) was a river in North Italy, "honoured" because Virgil was born near it.

Hippotades: Aeolus, the son of Hippotes; he controlled the winds.

Panope; a sea-nymph.

That sanguine flower inscribed with woe: the hyacinth. Hyacinthus was a Spartan prince who was accidently killed by Apollo. The Greeks declared that this flower had sprung from his blood and that they could trace the words "ai, ai" (alas! alas!) on its petals.

Rathe: Spenserian word meaning "early."

the Vision of the guarded mount: the apparition of the Archangel Michael is supposed to occupy at intervals the craggy seat of St. Michael's Mount, opposite the town of Marazion, near Land's End.

Namancos and Bayona: two places near Cape Finisterre in Spain. It was popularly imagined that they could be seen in a direct line from Land's End.

ON THE MORNING OF CHRIST'S NATIVITY

It seems almost incredible that this ode was written while Milton was only twenty-one years of age and still at Cambridge. It was begun very early in the morning of Christmas Day 1629, and it breathes the

Christmas spirit throughout, in its grandeur, loftiness of tone and majesty of sound, though it must be confessed it misses the beautiful simplicity connected in most human minds with the Christ-Child.

The stanza in the Hymn is Milton's own invention, though based on a type used by Spenser, and is particularly effective in its artistic pattern. At the end of every sixth line there is a strong pause, and the remaining two lines give the impression of a final couplet rounding off the verse. The whole effect of balance is greatly heightened by the interposition of five-feet lines among three-feet lines, and by the fact that the seventh line contains four feet and the last line is an Alexandrine. Numbering the lines we have 1 and 2 with three feet, 3 with five feet, 4 and 5 with three feet, 6 with five feet, 7 with four feet, and 8 with six feet. This metre, besides preserving the balance of the poem, prevents monotony and helps to impart an impression of pomp and grandeur, and gives a sense of chiming.

Other points which are particularly worthy of notice in the poem are the excellent combination of vowel-sounds, the greatest number being "open" vowels, *e.g.* "sweet" and "great," "steed" and "need," the frequent use of "liquid" consonants, *e.g.* "prolongs each heavenly close," the rhyme-scheme *aab, ccd, ee,* the musical use of proper names, such as Peor and Baalim and "moonèd Ashtaroth," the learning shown by the poet, the appropriate epithets, *e.g.* "prophetic cell," as well as the splendid imagery, especially in those verses describing the peacefulness of the night (verses 4 and 5 of the *Hymn*) and in the remarkable stanza dealing with the oracles (verse 19).

Milton was greatly interested in Italian writers, and this work was suggested by a poem written by Tasso. It begins in a low tone of hushed veneration, then the hymn seems to rise in grandeur until the climax is reached in the angels' song, then slowly falls to a quiet close. The *Introduction* begins by mentioning the birth of Christ (ll. 1-14) and closes by stating that the poet wishes to pay a tribute to the new-born Babe before the Wise Men arrive with their gifts (15-28). *The Hymn* begins by declaring that Nature clothes herself in a white garment of snow (ll 1.15), and shows that Peace heralds the coming of the Christ-child (15-25), that wars have ended (25-35), the winds have ceased from raging (36-40), the stars do not move (41-48), the sun hides his head (49-56), and the shepherds chat happily (57-66). Then the Heavenly music is heard (65-72). Its effect on Nature is shown (73-80) and the Heavenly choir is described (81-88) together with the type of music (89-104). Next comes a prophecy of the Golden Age, since Vanity and Sin will pass away and Truth and

Justice will return to mankind (105-120). The next portion of the poem explains why this cannot happen at once — Christ must suffer crucifixion (121-144). But the heathen gods know that their reign is coming to an end and they bewail their lost power — the Greek and Roman gods (145-169), the Syrian gods (170-182), the Egyptian gods (183-198) — all these are banished just as the sun drives away darkness (199-208). The last verse (209-216) shows the Christ-Child asleep, with stars and angels in attendance.

Oracles: the utterances of pagan deities. Such deities were consulted very often on matters of interest, and the answers (given, of course, by the priests) were generally ambiguous. The most famous oracle was that of Apollo at Delphi.

Lars: good spirits of the dead who may wander on this earth.

Lemures: evil spirits of the dead who wander about finding no rest.

Peor: Baal, a Syrian deity (male).

Baalim: Syrian gods — the plural form of Baal.

Ashtaroth: a Syrian deity (female).

Lybic Hammon: an oracle found in Lybia, often represented in the shape of a ram. Also called Ammon.

Thammuz: a Syrian god of Nature. Each spring the Syrian or Tyrian girls used to hold festivals to celebrate his supposed birth.

Moloch: Syrian god of the sun.

Isis: an Egyptian goddess, wife of Osiris, the chief Egyptian deity.

Orus: son of Osiris and Isis.

Osiris: chief Egyptian deity, represented by a bull, as Isis is represented by a cow.

ON HIS BEING ARRIVED AT THE AGE OF TWENTY-THREE

This sonnet was written in 1631, just before Milton's life at Cambridge ended. His birthday was on December 9th, so it was very probably written in that month. A friend some time later suggested to him that it was time he took up some definite work. Milton courteously replied in a letter enclosing the sonnet which stated that he had already given this matter some thought and realised that all his studies apparently led to no purpose but felt in his inmost mind that he was being led by Time and the will of Heaven to take up some very high vocation. Therefore he was willing to submit himself to whatever was in store for him, conscious that his patience would be rewarded and that he would win the approval of God.

The form of the sonnet is Petrarchan, the rhyme-scheme being *abba, abba, cde, dce.*

subtle thief: the thief that steals one's years away without one's noticing their passing.

no bud or blossom sheweth: gives no indication of my fitness for any work.

Perhaps my semblance might deceive the truth: Milton looked very young when he was at College and was known as "the lady of Christ's."

Inward ripeness doth much less appear: the maturity of mind and spirit which is found in some people seems to be less noticeable in me even than physical maturity.

timely-happy spirits: people who are happy and fortunate in accordance with their time of life.

endueth: endoweth. The word is connected with "dowry," — a gift.

be it less or more: whether it is less or more.

Task-Master: a reference to the parable of the labourers in the vineyard (Matthew xx.)

ON THE DEATH OF A FAIR INFANT DYING OF A COUGH

This is probably the first original English poem written by Milton. The infant referred to is the daughter of his sister Ann and Edward Phillips. It is a religious elegy, full of sincere feeling, despite all the strained imagery and stilted mythological allusions. The rhetoric characteristic of the seventeenth century cannot obscure the delightful passages here, especially the fifth stanza which treats of the theme of immortality. The poem suggests the later Milton of the serious, humorless disposition. The language and style are Spenserian rather than metaphysical in the Donne manner. The stanza has seven lines, rhyming a b a b b c c with a final Alexandrine.

ON THE DETRACTION WHICH FOLLOWED UPON MY WRITING CERTAIN TREATISES

This sonnet and the one which follows are sometimes said to show that Milton held rather loose views about the sanctity of marriage, but it should be remembered that both were written after 1645 when his wife had returned to him. He certainly had in certain pamphlets on Divorce put forward the idea that if a man and his wife could not agree they ought to be free to remarry after a public ceremony which would be equivalent to a decree of divorce. In this sonnet, however, he tries (rather unsuccessfully) to be humorous at the expense of his detractors who, he suggests, are very ignorant men and, far from understanding what his views on divorce were, do not even realise the meaning of "Tetrachordon." In fact they cannot pronounce the word correctly. Milton, when his wife deserted him in 1643, wrote four pamphlets on Divorce. These were (1) *The Doctrine and Discipline of Divorce Restored;* (2) *The Judgment of Martin Bucer concerning Divorce;* (3) *Tetrachordon, or Expositions upon the four chief places in Scripture which treat of Marriage;* (4) *Colasterion or a Reply to Nameless Answer against the Doctrine and Discipline of Divorce.*

The sonnet is especially concerned with the third of these.

Tetrachordon: A Greek word meaning "with four strings"; it was connected with four passages of Scripture: — (a) Genesis i and ii; (b) Deuteronomy xxiv; (c)Matthew v and xix; (d) Epistle to the Corinthians vii.

woven close, both matter, form, and style: Milton's power in close reasoning (matter) skilful arrangement of his ideas (form) and scholarly diction (style) is here well suggested.

the subject new: Divorce was seldom discussed or written about at that time.

numbering good intellects: attracting those readers who were clever enough to understand it.

now seldom pored on: very infrequently read now — as the novelty has worn off.

in file: one behind another — probably looking over one another's shoulders.

Mile End Green: a district in London.

Gordon: Lord George Gordon fought under Montrose on behalf of King Charles; he was slain in battle.

Colkitto, Macdonnel, Galasp: A Scotsman named Alexander Macdonald really owned all these names. He was the son of Colkittoch (which is a Scots word meaning "left-handed"), and the grandson of Galasp or Gillespie. Milton says in this sonnet that it is stupid of people not to be able to pronounce "Tetrachordon" because it is really harder to pronounce than "Gordon," "Colkitto," "Macdonald" or "Galasp."

grow sleek: do not sound at all difficult.

our like mouths: mouths like ours.

Quintilian: a Roman writer (A.D. 40-118) who paid great attention to style. Milton's idea here is that Quintilian would have thought these Scots names sounded very unmusical.

Thy age, like ours . . hated not learning: The age in which you lived did not hate learning as our age seems to do.

Sir John Cheek: A Cambridge professor of Greek who taught Edward VI. He was interested in the work of Greek and Roman writers, and in various branches of learning. His name was particularly well-known to Milton because he was connected with a Commission dealing with Divorce.

ON THE SAME

This sonnet deals with the same subject as the preceding one; but whereas the former was meant to be humorous this is written in a vein of bitterness. It is of the Petrarchan type the rhyme-scheme being *abba, abba, cdd, cde.*

to quit their clogs: to give up those ideas that hinder divorce.

the known rules of ancient liberty: those rules that were suggested by the Law of Moses and by the practice of the Early Church before ecclesiastical and other laws cast a restraint upon the liberty of the individual.

barbarous noise: a clamour raised by barbarians.

of owls and cuckoos, asses, apes and dogs: all these have unmusical cries.

those birds that were transformed to frogs, etc.: Ovid in the Metamorphoses told how Latona, who was beloved by Jupiter but hated by Juno, was compelled, owing to Juno's anger, to wander from one place to another, taking with her the twins Apollo and Diana. When she reached a small lake she, being very thirsty and fatigued, tried to drink, but the country-folk just laughed at her and made the water muddy by stirring it up with their hands and feet. Jupiter was so angry at this treatment that he turned them into frogs.

held the sun and moon in fee: Apollo was the God of the Sun and Diana the Goddess of the Moon.

in fee: absolutely. A legal term denoting unconditional possession.

this is got by casting pearl to hogs: this is the result of casting pearls before swine. A reference to Matthew vi, verse 6.

Licence they mean when they cry Liberty: a remark taken almost directly from "Tetrachordon."

who loves that: whoever loves Liberty.

from that mark how far they rove: how far they miss that mark. A reference to archery.

for: notwithstanding.

all this waste of wealth and loss of blood: the poverty and death caused by the Civil War.

ON THE RELIGIOUS MEMORY OF MRS. CATHERINE THOMSON, MY CHRISTIAN FRIEND, DECEASED DECEMBER 16, 1646

There are two theories about the lady to whom Milton has given this personal tribute of affection. One is that she was a relation of a landlord with whom Milton had rooms in London when he was Latin Secretary to the Commonwealth, the other that she was the wife of George Thomson, a London publisher and one of Milton's intimate friends. She was evidently a woman of excellent culture and character. The sonnet is Petrarchan in form, the rhyme-scheme being *abba, abba, cdcdcd.*

earthly load of death: a reference to the Epistle to the Romans, vii, 24, "who shall deliver me from the body of this death?"

from life doth sever: separates us from eternal or true life.

good endeavour: good works, c.f. Revelation, xiv. 13. "Their works do follow them."

golden rod: Faith is here represented as pointing the way to heaven by means of a golden rod. In poetry and in pictures saints are often shown holding rods.

knew them best thy handmaids: knew them, i.e. thy works to be thy handmaids.

ON THE LATE MASSACRE IN PIEDMONT

This is one of the mightiest of Milton's sonnets. As is usual with Milton it is of the Italian type, but the pause comes, not at the eighth line, but in the middle of the tenth, and the break in the thought is not very distinct. The open "o" vowels give a sense of continued sorrow and moaning. Milton's righteous indignation was aroused by the action of the Turin Government against the Protestant inhabitants of the Piedmontese valleys. In 1655 these people, known as the Vaudois or Waldensians, were ordered to conform to the Roman Catholic religion or else leave their homes within a very few days on pain of death. When they resisted this decree a massacre, accompanied by frightful atrocities, was carried out with the consent and connivance of the Duke of Savoy. Cromwell sent letters, which were written in Latin by Milton, to the offending Duke, demanding the withdrawal of the cruel edict, and the sum of £40,000 was subscribed for the relief of the sufferers. The result was that they were allowed to return to their valleys and carry on their own type of Protestant worship.

Piedmontese: the soldiers of the Duke of Savoy, who carried out the massacre.

Babylonian woe: Rome and Babylon were often identified in the writings of Puritans.

ON HIS BLINDNESS

This is one of the most personal of Milton's sonnets. He became totally blind in 1653, at the age of 45, but continued to act as Secretary to the Commonwealth until 1658. The thought changes in the middle of the sonnet from intense grief to the realisation that the impairment of his vision need not prove a handicap in his service for God. The language used is very simple; lines 2 and 11 are composed entirely of monosyllables, and there are no very learned words or difficult constructions. The metaphors in lines 10 and 13 are particularly apt.

ON HIS DECEASED WIFE

This sonnet refers to Milton's second wife Catherine Woodcock, and was probably written in 1658. He was apparently very fond of her and was heartbroken when she died in 1657, fifteen months after their marriage.

espoused: married.

Alcestis: the wife of Admetus, king of Pheræ in Thessaly. Admetus forgot to offer a sacrifice to Artemis, a goddess connected with marriage, on his wedding day, and accordingly was fated to die immediately. However Apollo asked the Fates to grant Admetus deliverance from death and they promised this if some member of his family would be willing to die in his stead. His wife Alcestis promised to do this and accordingly descended into Hades, but Hercules, who was a great friend of Admetus, went to the lower world and brought her back again to her husband.

old law: the Mosaic Law.

Her face was veiled: there is a suggestion here that Milton had never seen his wife's face, but had not met her until after he had become blind.

ON THE NEW FORCERS OF CONSCIENCE UNDER THE LONG PARLIAMENT

This is what is known as a "tailed" sonnet, that is a true sonnet of fourteen lines plus a tail or "coda" of six lines. Italian sonnets are sometimes written in this way, following quite strict poetic rules. The rhyme-scheme is *abba, abba, cde, dec, cff, fgg.*

In 1642 Parliament resolved that the Church ought not to be governed by Archbishops and Bishops, but it was not until 1646 that an ordinance abolishing them was passed. Then the Presbyterians in Parliament said that not only should "prelates" be abolished, but all religious sects that were not in sympathy with the Presbyterian form of Church Government should be suppressed. Milton, as an Independent, was violently opposed to this and accused the Presbyterians of being "the new forcers of Conscience." In this sonnet he asks, though perhaps in a rather harsh way, for toleration and religious liberty.

Prelate Lord: the "prelates" were the Archbishops and Bishops.

staff vows: definite decisions.

renounced his Liturgy: given up the Episcopal form of service based on the book of Common Prayer. "Liturgy" comes from a Greek word meaning "public service."

To seize the widowed whore Plurality: to sin by trying to hold some of the Church endowments which had been left (widowed) when the prelates were removed from holding them. Plurality means the holding of more than one ecclesiastical living. In the time of Charles I some vicars had

had two or three parishes, sometimes long distances apart, they could not possibly under these circumstances carry out their parochial duties profitably. Milton says the Presbyterian ministers are simply taking over these parishes for themselves and are still, therefore, "Pluralists."

whose sin ye envied, not abhorred: you did not condemn these priests who indulged in the sin of "plurality," you were simply envious of them.

adjure the civil sword: call upon the Civil Power, i.e. Parliament.

ride: over-ride.

classic hierarchy: "classic" has two meanings here (1) it is used in an ironic sense to mean "of the highest class"; (2) it refers to the "classes," i.e. the small Presbyterian Courts that were set up in each parish. "Hierarchy literally means "sacred rule," it is taken here to mean "government by priests."

A.S.: Adam Stewart a Scottish Presbyterian who wrote pamphlets attacking the Independents. His pamphlets were published under the initials A.S.

Rutherford: another Presbyterian of Scottish descent who published pamphlets against the Presbyterians. He was a minister and a member of the Westminster Assembly which wanted to impose on England a Presbyterian type of religion. He also held the post of professor of Divinity at the University of Saint Andrews.

mere: this word is designed to express contempt for these Presbyterians.

intent: intentions.

Paul: Milton wishes to infer that the Apostle Paul was a good preacher.

heretics: this word now means "people who are opposed to widely-accepted opinion," but in Milton's day it meant "those who make their own choice."

shallow Edwards: "shallow" like "mere" is used to express contempt. The Rev. Thomas Edwards, a London preacher who had turned from being an Anglican to a Presbyterian, had attacked the independents in general and Milton in particular in a pamphlet.

Scot What-d'ye-call: Milton is here possibly referring to the Rev. Robert Baillie, Professor of Divinity in the University of Glasgow, who had in 1645 attacked Milton for his views on divorce. The poet is here expressing contempt for his opponent by suggesting that he cannot even remember his opponent's name.

packing: schemes, especially schemes for securing undue advantage for one side over another.

Trent: The Council of Trent in Austria-Hungary which existed from 1545 to 1563 was held to attempt to check the progress of the Reformation. From this Council Protestants were excluded so only one side of a question was ever heard, i.e. the side showing the arguments of the Roman Catholics. Milton suggests that the Westminster Assembly was an equally unfair Council because it excluded the Independents.

with their wholesome and preventive shears: by cutting off your power as if with a pair of shears.

Clip your phylacteries: check your pretensions to great goodness. The Pharisees, who pretended to be particularly holy, used to wear slips of parchment bearing passages of Scripture on their foreheads or their left arms, these were called phylacteries. They are referred to in St. Matthew's Gospel, xxiii, 5, "make broad their phylacteries."

baulk your ears: cheat your ears what they ought to suffer, i.e. mutilation. In Milton's day mutilation was sometimes carried out. Thus William Prynne, a Presbyterian, had his nose and ears cut off for writing against the Church and the theatre.

succour our just fears: take away our justifiable fears from us.

in your charge: as an accusation against you.

New Presbyter is but old Priest writ large: the new Presbyterians are even worse and more intolerant than the Episcopalians used to be. "Priest" is really the shortened form of "Presbyter" which comes from a Greek word meaning "elder."

ON THE UNIVERSITY CARRIER

Old Hobsen died, and the carrier inspires Milton to write one of his rare, lightly humorous pieces. It is an epigram full of puns and conceits characteristic of the day. Hobsen may have been an object of ridicule when alive, but now the author realizes he was a nice chap after all.

ON TIME

This ode expresses Milton's deep love for music and its inspirational effects. Again the idea of the harmony of the spheres is present. The rhyme is irregular, as in *At a Solemn Music*.

ON SHAKESPEARE

This criticism of Shakespeare chimes in with the other estimates that considered Shakespeare great, but wanting in art. Milton uses a metaphysical conceit in which he suggests that Shakespeare creates for himself a monument by turning his readers to stone. The Bard's genius is one of natural origin, rather than that of the deliberate, conscious artist.

PARADISE LOST

A. The Evolution of Paradise Lost

This is the crowning jewel of Milton's career. From his earliest years, Milton had plans and ambitions to create a literary masterpiece that would remain imperishable. Time and time again, he had expressed a desire to write an epic poem in English comparable in theme and manner to the great epics of Greece and Rome. In *Vacation Exercise* we have a first hint of his ambition; he has no ideas as yet of any specific subject or theme. Again the epic form is envisioned in *Elegy VI,* in which Milton sides with serious epic poetry as against light verse. Although in *Mansus* and in *Epitaphium Damonis* he speaks of the Arthurian episodes as good material for an epic, he shows further doubt about the matter in the prose *Reason of Church Government.* In *Lycidas,* as we have seen, the poet is dissatisfied with his subjects, and he considers the pastoral form he uses in the elegy as a bridge to the epic form to come.

An interesting plan of subjects for epic or dramatic treatment is drawn up by Milton soon after he returns from Italy. He sets down here a large list of about a hundred subjects suitable for treatment, most of them based on Biblical history or the history of England. Some are just mentioned; others have been outlined in detail. Although the subjects are slated for use in drama, it is not likely that another list, not found, contains similar subjects of epic themes. In this list the main subject is no longer an interest in King Arthur; it is, rather, a preoccupation with the fall of man. There are even four different drafts on the subject of the Fall, and these drafts are the first real move in the direction of the writing of *Paradise Lost.* Remember, however, that all this was to be in play form as yet. In these drafts much of the philosophic purport of *Paradise Lost* is stated, as well as many of the characters of the epic.

Why Milton changed his plan of writing a drama to creating an epic is not clear. Perhaps one reason was the bigness and movement of the subject, too complicated to be produced in a few hours on a stage. Also, the closing of the threatres in 1642 may have influenced his decision. Anyway, Milton finally seemed to believe that his purposes would best be served by an epic. The actual writing of the work may have started either in 1655 or 1657. However, John Aubrey, basing his decision on what Edward Phillips had told him, said the poem was started in 1658. Aubrey also said that the poem was finished in 1663. Publication, however, was definitely in 1667; it was printed in ten books first, and in 1674, in twelve books, since Milton had decided to divide Book VII and Book X into two books each.

B. The Cosmography of Paradise Lost

Milton's epic takes place everywhere; in Heaven, Hell, and on Earth. There were quite a few systems, astronomical systems, that attempted in his day to explain the structure of the universe. Although he knew of the Copernican system, a system that appealed most strongly to the leading scholars and scientists of the day, he decided to base his imaginative vision of the universe on the more traditional Ptolemaic system. He believed that the Ptolemaic conception of the universe was fixed in the minds of the people through ages of theological and literary interpretation. Moreover, he was through his studies, especially familiar with this system and its mathematical details. The Ptolemaic theory presents us with the earth in the center, and all the astronomical bodies revolved around it. Milton, in his poem, held to the geocentric view as espoused by Plato and Dante. Some of the details of his structure of the universe are his own. A plan or diagram of Milton's world might be as follows:

Space is divided into Heaven or the Empyrean on top, and Chaos, or matter not yet created, on the bottom. Just below Chaos, God created Hell. Out of Chaos, God also created the world, or the Earth and the spheres. Earth is fixed at the center, and around it move concentric spheres, ten of them, the Moon, Mercury, Venus, the Sun, Mars, Jupiter, Saturn, the sphere of the fixed stars, the Crystalline sphere, and the Primum Mobile, the latter serving to move the rest. In complications, and in the ability to make clear these complications, Milton has no rival except Dante.

C. Outline of Paradise Lost

BOOK I

This book begins as do all epics of tradition, *in medias res,* in the middle of the story, with a precise statement of the theme of the epic. The theme is the fall of man as seen in Adam, the representative of the race itself. The purpose of the poem is to show the justice of God's handling of the whole situation, "to justify the ways of God to man." After calling on the Muse, Urania, for divine inspiration, he starts the story proper with a description of Satan raising his hand on the burning lake, after he had been expelled from Heaven by God and the angels. For nine days he lay groveling in Hell. Here Satan sees "No light; but rather darkness visible."

Near him he sees the Prince of Devils, Beelzebub. Satan, a proud mind, says defiantly that, despite his fall, he is still unrepentant and still affirms his "high disdain from sense of injured merit." To Beelzebub (and the fallen angels whom he has carried from heaven with him) he says:

> "What though the field be lost?
> All is not lost — the unconquerable will,
> And study of revenge, immortal hate,
> And courage never to submit or yield."

Satan expresses his hatred of God and his desire for revenge. He glories in the fact that he even dared to battle with God, and he emphasizes his determination never to stop until he is successful.

God he no longer thinks of as divine, but seething with the same evil passions he himself has. He thinks that he is as great as God; that the angels were created by Fate as equals to God, and owe him no submission. Satan is indeed heroically courageous, but he is also basically evil and gifted with the ability to lie persuasively. Beelzebub does not think that the condition of the angels, all suffering in the burning lake, is at all favorable to the determination of Satan to resist and persist. He is disheartened at the prospect of further battle and struggle, and believes that future attempts will end in further defeat. Satan scorns such pessimism; he opposes God's will adamantly, and swears to carry on warfare forever, if necessary, in a struggle between Good and Evil. He even welcomes the lower regions of Hell as his home, and asserts that the mind, or soul, has the power to overcome the environment in which it finds itself, and can make a Heaven of Hell. At least, in Hell he and his crew are free, subject to no overlordship. He makes a speech to his followers, rouses them to action, and promises them his leadership in the battles to come. He imparts into their beaten spirits some of the magic of his own indomitable courage.

These angels, these rebel angels, are all lying in a fiery gulf surrounded by a "darkness visible," tortured by fire. Soon, under the encouragement of Satan, they rise in the burning plain and assemble before their leader. Just as Homer uses in the *Iliad* a catalogue of all the ships and heroes of the war, so Milton enumerates here the various legions and their leaders — Moloch, Chemos, Astoreth, Dagon, Belial, etc., — idols and false gods of all climes and races. Satan then addresses them once more, and tells them Heaven can yet be regained, if they wish it. He reveals, furthermore, that a new world is to be created by God in which a new kind of creature will be housed. He will hold a council to determine what is the nature of this new world and its creatures, and how they could thwart God's plans. His audience is aroused to action, and they begin to build a palace called Pandemonium, where the Peers are to sit in council. With terrific industry, the angels build a kind of Doric temple. Since all of the hosts cannot, in their natural great size, fit into the council hall, a miracle takes place in which the masses of the army are transformed into the size of pygmies, the leaders, however, retaining their original mammoth proportions. The meeting is called to order, and the consultation begins.

BOOK II

Book I had been mainly narrative and descriptive in presentation. This book has more of a dramatic conflict, of character and situation.

The book opens with a masterful debate in the council, a debate which Milton had no doubt seen and heard during the trying days of the Revolution. Perhaps some the leading lights of the political arena of his day were the models for his debaters in Pandemonium. The eloquence with which the debate is carried on is the glory of Book II, and Satan, as ever, is the predominating voice of the assembly, allowing, it is true, the voicing of individual opinions, but seeing to it that his views and his will prevail. That all of the fallen angels are agreed as to the need of revenge and rehabilitation Satan takes for granted at once as he starts the meeting. The only real question is what means to use. Should it be secret spying and treachery, or war waged in the open? Two speakers, who represent opposite tendencies of statesmen in public life, argue the question. The first, Moloch, is definitely determined to support military attack at once. His speech is to the point, forceful and brief. His opponent, Belial, has a more subtle, polished delivery, coming to grips with the subject deviously, but surely. He advises a policy of peaceful conduct, so that they can all relax and enjoy whatever they can in this infernal region. Possibly we can read into both these prescriptions of policy the nationalistic supporter of war and destruction and the easy-going advocate of peace on any terms whatsoever. Another speaker, Mammon, supports Belial's advice, for the most part, and states further that, instead of waging war, they should exploit Hell itself, make the best of the resources they have, and so get accustomed to their new habitation. The crowd seems to be swayed towards his views, and Satan is afraid that he will be outvoted. Beelzebub, however, rises to the occasion in support of his leader. He is a subtle political manipulator, and swerves the masses away from Mammon's plans. He reminds them that a new world is being born that has people in it and that is open to attack from without. Here is an opportunity to wreak revenge without too much loss of safety, and also the likelihood of seizing new wealth. The council agrees by almost unanimous vote. Who is to carry out the dangerous mission to search out this new world and explore its possibilities? Satan forestalls debate by volunteering and thus he gains, even more than before, the admiration and respect of his comrades.

After the meeting is over, the angelic hosts satisfy the needs of the individual for play and recreation. Those of higher standing engage in poetry and music; those still higher attempt to discuss philosophical questions; the lower classes merely participate in physical relaxation, games and sports of all kinds. Some are more practical, and begin exploring the phenomena and boundaries of the new regions into which they were hurled. Milton suggests here that, although, as angels, they have the intellectual equipment to cope with all problems, still, as evil, fallen angels, they are devoid of truth and virtue and love, and thus find no solutions to their problems, but wander in circles, lost in their tarnished glory.

Abruptly the story turns to Satan and his journey. There follows a vivid, if rather horrible, section that describes the meeting with Sin and Death. Sin is Satan's daughter, as well as his harlot, in Heaven, and Death is their son. Sin and Death are guardians of the gates of Hell. Sin is obeying the commands of God not to open the gates, but Satan, persuasive as usual, makes her open these and now the coast is clear. He begins his spectacular journey through the realms of Chaos, the uncreated and confused regions; Chaos himself directs him, until, swimming valiantly through the terrific pressures of the region, he enters finally into the vicinity of the new world, into a region pervaded by light and peace and order. Milton's descriptions here are a revelation of unparalleled imaginative resources.

BOOK III

With the scene now changed to Heaven and its characters, there is a falling off of literary and inspirational powers, a decline to be expected when one deals with the intangible of perfection and virtue. The book opens with an invocation to God in which Milton becomes personal in his revelation of feelings. He speaks of the greatness of light, of his own blindness, his desire for fame, and his deathless love of beauty. If he is denied physical light, at least he is conscious of inner light, inner virtue and vision. There follows a stiff, formal, dignified dialogue in Heaven between God and His Son, or Christ, in which Milton's theological ideas are expressed. God knows that Satan is flying to the new World, and he can, even now, predict that he, Satan, will succeed in wrecking the new region and its inhabitants. Man, however, will be perverted by Satan, even though he has the free will to resist temptation. God had created man with the ability and the will to choose; God is not to blame for Man's final choice. But since Man is to fall, not by malicious intention, but by temptation from without, God will be merciful towards him; the Son is touched at the plight of Man. God's decree that Man must die for his sins, unless someone can take on his punishment and answer for his sins, stimulates Christ to offer himself as a sacrifice. God is glad, and there follows a demonstration in which all the angels join in tribute to the Son's courage.

Back turns the scene to Satan, who is now alighting on the convex of the new World, and, for the first time, he sees the great beauties of the earth or paradise. There intervenes a passage in which Milton describes the Limbo of Vanity or the Paradise of Fools, and here he exhibits his anti-Catholic bias rather unnecessarily. Satan meets the archangel of the Sun, Uriel, who, tricked by a new disguise that Satan puts on, directs him to Mount Nephates.

BOOK IV

In this book, Milton returns to the peak of creativity reached in Books I and II. This is a dramatic opening, Satan in the new World, envious, passionately evil and regretful. His speech recalls his former greatness in Heaven and his abject condition now. Gone is much of his former boastful confidence. Hell is in his soul now. Now he determines to accept as his good, his God, evil itself. Notice that as Satan becomes torn with conflicting passions, he undergoes a change in appearance. A magnificent description follows of the Garden of Eden. This description is ornate, Elizabethan, luxuriant in its details and replete with allusions to classical sources. So charming, so beautiful, is the Garden, and so noble in figure the naked parents, Adam and Eve, that even Satan is for the moment enveloped in pity. But this momentary reappearance of his former angelic character is counteracted by the envious emotions that Satan feels and by his original plan and purpose to seduce Man, and thus indirectly revenge himself on God.

Adam and Eve in their conversation exhibit almost perfect natures and connubial bliss. Adam is grateful for the delights of the Garden, and he recalls God's commands not to eat of the fruit of the for- bidden tree. Eve recalls her birth, her meeting with Adam, the reflection of herself in the pool — all with a frank, innocent, but charming manner. Her Narcissus-like enchantment with her own beauty is mentioned here, I believe, to prepare the reader with the later downfall of Eve, as she allows her own vanity to cause the catastrophe.

Uriel, meanwhile, noticing the change in the appearance of Satan, becomes suspicious, and he warns the angelic guard. Adam and Eve are depicted in the throes of domestic bliss and married love in their nuptial chamber. Milton celebrates ideal domestic happiness, both spiritual and physical. Chivalric love he is against, with its false ideals and hypocritical actions. The only kind of real love is to be found in a marriage in which both parties esteem each other. Woman is not to be put on a pedestal; she is to be conscious of the superiority of her mate, intellectually and otherwise. He exists "for God only," she "for God in him." Milton's conception of the inferiority of woman to man is not, however, one in which the female is totally dependent. She has a will of her own, and she has an important function, other than mere creation, to assume in the domestic relationship.

Advised of Satan's treachery, the angels surprise Satan at night close to the ear of Eve as she is asleep, tempting her in a dream. They bring him to Gabriel, who questions him further. Satan's answers are scornful and deceptive, and before some altercation can ensue, a sign from Heaven, the scales of Justice weighing against Satan, intervenes. Satan flies at once out of Paradise.

BOOK V

In the morning, Eve tells Adam of the disturbing dream she had, unaware that it was Satan who had been tormenting her mind in sleep. Adam gives her a lecture on the causes and effects of dreams, ending by comforting her with the thought that evil ideas, unconsciously perceived and unapproved, do not reflect censure on the dreamer, and are just fleeting. There follows a morning hymn or prayer before they begin their day's work — a hymn that eulogizes the glory of God and the bounty of Nature through Him. In this hymn, Milton's Hebraic lore and Hebraic understanding come to the fore. God now sends Raphael down to warn the pair of the possible temptations of evil and of the need of obeying God's commands. An interesting discussion follows on the differences of angelic and human natures. Angels are like humans, but differ only in degree. Like humans, angels have a body that functions similarly, but everything is on a higher plane or scale, and much more ethereal or refined. Body and soul, spirit and matter are not essentially different, one mixing with the other.

Raphael continues his talk by supporting the belief in the freedom of the will and then describes the rebellion of Lucifer, or Satan, and his followers. In the epics of the past, we also had stories within a story, like the tale of Aeneas related to Dido. Adam and Eve now are fully instructed; they know which is good or evil. Raphael, who had been treated as a guest with the proper hospitality, continues the story of the fall; he tells of the lone rebel, Abdiel, a Seraph, who refused to join the conspiracy against God, who dared to argue against Satan and oppose his authority, and who finally leaves the dissenting party. Milton intends Adam to perceive the analogy between earth and Heaven. Earth is merely a shadow or "idea" (platonically speaking) of the region of Heaven. Abdiel, also, by his conduct, could exemplify the man of ethical principles and moral fortitude who, because of these qualities, can withstand by himself the pressures of society against his inner convictions.

BOOK VI

This is the book that relates the battle scenes between God and Satan's forces. God's lieutenants, Michael and Gabriel, force Satan, after the first day's battle, to retire at night. In the council called by Satan, horrible weapons and engines of destruction are devised, and, on the second day, it is Satan who scores against God's forces first. For defense, the angelic hosts hurl mountains at the enemy, and soon overcome them, so that, on the third day, God provides the finishing touch by selecting His Son, the Messiah, to handle them. He alone with His Chariot and thunder for support drives the enemy to destruction, forcing them to leap down into the abyss of Hell. The Messiah returns as the conquering hero.

Milton relied on military books for his account of the technical aspects of war. He shows the bestiality, confusion, and purpose-lessness of war in his account of a battle in which armies fight like Titans, now bold, now vicious, now abandoning mere arms and using whatever weapons are at hand. God must put a stop to this insane brutality and chaos, and so He sends His Son to the fray. Perhaps it is awkward, artistically, to read of angels, superior spirits, engaging in such brawls, but if Heaven is only another Earth, but raised to bigness, Nature, refinement, and endurance, then Milton's story is properly apropos.

BOOK VII

Adam wants to know of the creation of the world. Raphael tells him of God's desire to create a new region and new people. All this is prefaced by another invocation, this time one that reflects the isolation of Milton himself amid the era known as the Restoration, a period in English history filled with spiritual and physical attitudes extremely distasteful to him. Raphael's account of the creation follows pretty closely the account in the Bible, in Genesis. Although Milton adds details of his own, he keeps close to the original. Ornate and multiform in variety is the description of the creation of birds, fishes, animals, and, finally, Man. After this Herculean task is over, a six-day labor, psalms of rejoicing and gratitude are sung by the angels, continuing their song even through the Sabbath. Their music has overtones of thought which hint at the good that will follow the defeat of evil. God was great in his defeat of the angels;

he is greater in his creative powers, in his ability to create life and order out of chaos. It is better and greater to create than to destroy. Peace is better than war, and Milton, all through his work, has never failed to emphasize this fact, in his sonnets, his prose, and in his own conduct in public life.

BOOK VIII

When Adam, already appraised of the beginnings of evil in the universe, and of the punishments of the perpetrators of evil, asks Raphael about celestial motions, he receives a quiet rebuke. Matters like these are too far beyond man's legitimate sphere or limit of natural curiosity. Raphael warns Adam to think only of "what concerns thee and thy being." In other words, Milton is attacking here wild speculation and useless knowledge.

Adam reciprocates by telling Raphael of his own creation, his meeting with Eve, and the rest. The tale is delightful and needs no comment. Notice here Adam's dignity, his yearning for God and virtue, his belief in the omniscience of God, arrived at by himself through pure reasoning. By nature, too, he yearns for human fellowship, and accepts Eve as his mate, to be "one flesh, one heart, one soul." Adam's one weakness is hinted at here. He is powerless against the force of beauty. Raphael, at this point, warns Adam again of the will, of the freedom of choice, and that man must control his desires by the use of reason. Even angels can love, with wisdom, and Raphael gives us a description of the process — a rather unique and somewhat humorous episode. Raphael then repeats his warnings and leaves the lovers in their Paradise.

BOOK IX

With this book, Milton enters upon one of the most dramatic sections of Paradise Lost, the temptation and the fall. The book opens with a passage in which the poet compares his theme to that of the other established epics. In spiritual depth, his subject or theme is even more heroic than the others. Their themes were war and outward conflicts; his is profoundly religious and ethical and one of inward struggle. Calling on God's aid again, he continues his narrative with a description of Satan encircling the earth and finally entering Paradise disguised as a mist of the night. Satan soliloquizes again, noting his inferior position now, and marveling to what degree of baseness he will descend to seek revenge, a revenge he knows may even recoil on him. As he enters into the serpent's body and therein inbruting himself, his state of mind is one of bitter despair, even when he thinks he can succeed in his mission.

Adam and Eve, meanwhile, awake the next morning, and in a fresh dialogue, Eve, according to the best domestic traditions, has a plan by which they can accomplish more in their daily work; both should separate while gardening, so that no time will be wasted in talk. Adam, wiser as usual, warns that there is danger in being found alone, possibly, by an evil force or tempter. Eve is hurt to think that Adam does not trust her firmness and will, and a domestic squabble ensues. Milton is preparing the reader for the conclusion that Eve was responsible for what later happened, and that Adam tried vainly to stop her. Still Eve puts up a splendid argument, affirming that to be tempted only is not to be dishonored, and, besides, virtue, goodness, and truth can be tested only by trial. Adam does not force her to stay; he gives in, but most unwillingly. As they part, Milton gives us a lyrical, tender scene, in which the beauty of Eve is compared to the best in classical mythology. Even Satan cannot help admiring her. His seduction of Eve, which follows, is a most subtle piece of work. He uses, first, flattery, and makes Eve think more than before of her abilities and means. Eve hesitates before sinning but Satan presses home his purpose by uttering most forceful speeches, ridiculing the idea that a command can be so irrational as God's prohibition concerning the tree of knowledge. Besides, it is almost time for lunch, and Eve naturally is hungry. Milton sees to it that Eve is fully conscious that she is sinning.

Eve, however, convinces herself rather speciously by arguing for her right to eat of the forbidden fruit, in the vein used by Satan himself. She rationalizes her guilty act. When it is over, she acquires qualities not had before: selfishness, jealousy, and the like. What about Adam? She lies to him about the whole event. Adam knows he must not, and personally does not want to, eat of the fruit. But love, unreasonable love, or passion, prompts him to put himself in the same position as his beloved — and he also succumbs and feels the transitory delights of sin.

Now Adam and Eve are smitten by lustful desire, something not heretofore a part of their relationship. As a result, after the lustful act, disillusionment and dismay and remorse all set in and cause them both to quarrel and accuse each other. Now they know shame and disgust as well as lust. The whole episode is treated dramatically, and Milton's analysis of states of mind here is masterful from an artistic and psychological point of view. Note again that it is the woman who is most responsible for the fall, although Milton does not absolve Adam by any means.

BOOK X

God sends down His Son to judge the transgressors. The judgment is according to the sentence in the Book of Genesis: the expulsion from Paradise, the introduction of work and sorrow, and the woman's submission from now on to her husband's will. Sin and Death return to the narrative now, and ask Satan for a reward for their labors. The pair are now to dwell on earth and wield dominion over all nature. Satan, meanwhile, believing himself victorious, returns to his rebel hosts and boasts of his triumph. His happiness is short-lived, for soon 'after his vain-glorious speech, all the angels are turned into serpents and their applause turns to scornful hisses. Now this outward degradation is a manifestation of the degradation of their inner being.

Adam, meanwhile, laments the loss of his Paradise, and he falls into a state of extreme pessimism. He mourns the unpredictability of life and sin, and death, and of the mutability of things. Eve's regrets and lamentations take a different course here. She worries less about herself than of him. While Adam takes time to belabor woman's role in the universe, Eve exhibits tenderness, unselfishness, and poignant pity in her lamentations. She suggests, furthermore, that they could commit self-destruction rather than produce off-spring fated to struggle throughout their lives. Seeing his mate so dangerously low in spirits, Adam rallies and he courageously attempts to console her. Whereas Book IX ended with one spouse accusing the other, Book X closes with a religious appeal to God, and a reconciliation between themselves.

BOOK XI

Michael is to be the angelic minister of God's justice. God, after listening to the Son's appeal for mercy to the pair, insists that they must, nevertheless, leave Paradise. He instructs Michael to descend with a band of Cherubim and lead them out; also he tells Michael to foretell the future of the world to Adam. Adam is sensitive to some change by natural signs, the coming down of the angels with Michael, their leader. When Adam is informed of the decree of banishment he is speechless; Eve, however, finds voice in a heart-felt paean of lament at leaving all the beautiful surroundings she had tended with such loving care. When Adam says that now, perhaps he will no longer be able to communicate with God, Michael begins his story of the future, in an effort to prove to Adam that divine love and justice shall ever be present. The prophecy follows very carefully the story in the Bible, and is modelled after the sixth book of Virgil's

Aeneid, in which the Sybil predicts future Roman history. This story Milton uses also to show that the sins of the fathers are visited upon the children, at the same time that it exhibits God's eternal love and patience for humanity, exemplified by the salvation of man through Christ's sacrifice. The story will continue from here through Book XII. As a lesson in condensation alone, of the Hebrew books, it is a masterpiece. Book XI ends with the coming of the flood, and the appearance of the rainbow, at last, as a memento of God's mercy and grace.

BOOK XII

In Book XI, Michael related the story by showing Adam a succession of scenes to illustrate the various stages in history. Now his technique is not so patently visual; he appeals now to Adam's intellect, and tries to impress upon him the lessons, moral and spiritual, of the future history of the race. Adam realizes that all is not lost, for eventually Christ's sacrifice will restore the world's inhabitants to grace and happiness. Good shall finally conquer evil, just as Christ shall triumph over Satan. Adam vows to be patient and restrain his unlawful desires and obey God's laws. Michael agrees with Adam, and exhorts him to practice faith, love, and virtue. True happiness resides within the head, and there is man's real Paradise. Eve had not listened to all this, for she was asleep. Awakened, she joins Adam and Michael in the exit from Paradise, refreshed by a beautiful dream that had foretold to her final deliverance. The pair leave Paradise with mingled feelings; sadness, because of the beauty they are leaving, and hope, hope for the future and its rewards as well as its struggles.

D. Philosophic Significance

Tomes could be written of the various intellectual ramifications found in *Paradise Lost*. It contains matter for discussion in natural science, astrology, theology, ethics, politics, metaphysics, and the like. It is a vast storehouse of the learning of the period accumulated and made use of by a great scholar as well as a great poet. The poem deals with the nature of man and of God as well as with the different duties man must perform in all spheres of activity.

The theme of the book is explicitly stated: the Fall of Man. The moral purpose is to "justify the ways of God to man" and demonstrate that in life there is a purposeful, kindly superintendence by God, and that man's sufferings in life are the effects of man's own actions, not God's. Man had been given reason by God, the power to choose between good and evil. Man had freedom of will — that is a cardinal fact in Milton's philosophical and theological structure.

Although *Paradise Regained* had to follow to demonstrate explicitly the idea that by Christ's sacrifice mankind will be freed from the results of Adam's transgression, that idea is also stressed often in *Paradise Lost*. The latter, however, is concerned mainly with the origin of sin, Satan's revolt, his fall, his scheme against the married pair, their transgression and expulsion, and the promised hope of deliverance or redemption.

The characters, the main characters of the story, are symbolic of the great force of good and evil that dominate our lives. God, according to Milton, is eternal and carries on his eternity in his creation of the angels and the Son. Matter exists in the universe, but it is chaotic until God creates something thereof — until He gives it order and purpose. Satan and his rebellion are an introduction of confusion, and God creates another kind of being to make up for the loss of the faithful. Satan also has a certain freedom of will. By seducing Adam and Eve, Satan has introduced the problem of evil into the hitherto stable and orderly universe. Christ now fits perfectly into Milton's scheme of things. He must be the sacrificial agent for sinful humanity. Satan's insidious guile and pride are counteracted by Christ's mercy and humility, as well as courage. From now on, Christ and Satan will be antagonists throughout the history of the world until the final judgment day, Christ's second coming, when Satan will at last be everlastingly established in the lower regions.

Milton's ideas can be traced to various sources — to doctrines of Stoicism, Platonism, Catholicism, Puritanism. He was extremely stoical in his beliefs, in his emphasis on duty and responsibility. Yet he was also cognizant of the need for humility and obedience to God. From Plato, he inherited the dichotomy of reason and emotion or passion. Milton is a Christian idealist at heart, with strong strands of Stoic and Platonic thought. The theological content of his thought in *Paradise Lost,* although Catholic in many respects, may best be labeled a kind of reformed Catholicism, or Calvinism. He is in many respects definitely hostile to the accepted teachings of the Catholic Church.

E. Literary Sources
The following are probably Milton's leading sources used by Milton for his great epic:

1. The *Iliad, Odyssey,* and *Aeneid.*
2. The Bible, the Talmud, Rabbi Malmonides, Josephus.
3. St. Augustine, Du Bartas.
4. Hugo Gretius' *Adamus Exul,* Andreini's *L'Adamo,* Vendel's *Lucifer.*
5. Spenser, Shakespeare, Marlowe, and Giles and Phineas Fletcher.

Milton was a great reader and scholar, and as a matter of course his poem could not help being saturated with much of his literary and scientific knowledge. But he was no mere borrower. He assimilated what he read and transformed his borrowings by sifting them through the varied facets of his imagination. *Paradise Lost* is an original masterpiece, despite the debt Milton owed to predecessors.

F. Characterization

In the outline section of this paper a good deal has been said already about characterization. The minor characters are most interesting when they belong to Satan's group. *Beelzebub,* the perfect tool of his master, is a skilled politician who knows how to steer a proper course in debate. *Moloch* remains a soldier endowed with a brutal nature; *Belial* represents corruption and sloth, and *Mammon* is the prototype of the lover of material gain. The diviner characters are, by nature, less vivid or interesting. It is difficult to describe excellence unalloyed with faults. God is always right, and always majestic; but we do not enter wholeheartedly and emotionally into the delineation. Christ is also a formal, stiff portrait, representing theological ideas. *Raphael* is noted for his tender graciousness; *Michael,* on the contrary, is rather strict and pedantic. *Abdiel,* the rebel here against Satan's band who returns to God at last, may be a personification of Milton's own character — a righteous individual, undaunted by threats, and willing to remain alone in his convictions.

It is the three leading characters that Milton brings to life with unforgettable powers, Satan particularly. The latter is the epic hero par excellence. His attributes are varied; indomitable pride, unconquerable rebellion, will to evil and power, and insidious guile. He has a great driving force of his own, even if it lies in the direction of evil. There is a terrific drive in Satan, an adventurous daring that are endearing to the reader. As he pursues his course, he degenerates from the proud rebel of the first few books to the liar, perverter, cruel and envious seducer of the middle and later books. His superior endowments decline, until at last he becomes the lowly serpent.

In comparison with the forceful Satan, *Adam* pales into lesser significance. His role is by nature passive, not active. But he is an appealing figure as he symbolically stands for humanity. He is affectionate, tender, respectful of authority, willing to learn, solicitous of Eve. He is curious about himself and others, and his relationship to the universe. He is always desirious of participation in religious communion with God. It is true that his is a passionate nature, perhaps the one real weakness in Adam's armor, and this emotional power is responsible mainly for his submission to Eve in the fall. He knows intellectually he is doing wrong; but his consuming passion prompts him to partake of the apple. To us, this act has something of the heroic in it; but to Milton, to his mind, at least, the act was condemnatory. Notice the change in Adam after sinning; he argues falsely, he is lustful in his relations with Eve, he becomes pessimistic and despairing, cynical. But, unlike Satan, he returns through experience to a true realization of God's will and man's duties. At the end Adam is a grown, mature personality, not the slightly fanciful and blissfully happy person in Paradise.

Eve does not receive Milton's impartial judgment, although a good deal of sympathy is expressed for her. Before her sinning, she is the ideal mate or wife, possessing the necessary qualities of modesty, love, charm, and above all, the realization of Adam's superiority to her, mentally and physically. Her vanity is touching and pathetically expressed in her loving image reflected in the pool. Eve makes mistakes, of course; her desire to work alone in the garden, contrary to Adam's wishes, is indicative of stubbornness and wilfulness. When Satan is near her, she is a mere puppet. Her sensuality, her vanity, and her prying curiosity pave the way for her complete seduction. After the fall, she is at once lustful and selfish. She redeems herself later in her plea to be forgiven, and in her true remorse. She leaves us with a feeling of admiration for her heroic stand at the moment of exile from Eden. Milton has understood facets of the feminine mind and personality, and in Eve he gives us a convincing portrayal of that understanding.

G. Style

Whatever is said here of Milton's style is applicable not only to *Paradise Lost,* but also to much of his other work. Milton is a great stylist; of that there is no doubt. He is an innovator, an original practitioner of the grand style or manner in English poetry. It is an individual style, moulded not only by the requirements of his theme, but also by the bent of his temperament. Milton's style is different, far different from that of the Elizabethans. It is not a realistic manner of expression; instead, it is bookish, learned, recondite, Latinate, and highly intellectual. Whatever its merits, it is a succesful medium for the themes he chose to celebrate, achieving a sublimity and dignity never before and never again achieved in the language. It is not enough to say the style is "organ-toned," stately, sublime, and the like. Perhaps it would be wise to enumerate some definite characteristics. The verse, of course, is blank verse, English heroic verse without rhyme. His lines, although usually decasyllabic, are varied, with occasional light endings. The following characteristics are most prominent:

1. The natural order of word formations is usually inverted, with the subject often appearing at the end of the sentence, or the object standing first for emphasis.

2. Archaisms, obsolete phraseology, and Latinate vocabulary abound in his style.

3. Verbs used as nouns, and nouns as verbs; adjectives used as nouns or even adverbs.

4. Frequent omissions of words not strictly needed to convey the general meaning.

5. The use of apposition and frequent parentheses.

6. Tendency to use proper names, foreign and recondite, with sounds that lend dignity to his style.

7. Like the Greek epic poet, Homer uses compound epithets most frequently.

8. The habit of inserting between the natural subject and predicate of his sentence many other clauses and phrases that impede the progress of the sense of the sentence until it is over. This is called *suspension*.

9. A richness of imagery. Not a careful observation of the minutiae of nature, but rather a vivid comprehension of nature in general, its large aspects. Appeals to the senses, especially the sense of sound and the sense of smell.

10. The use of the epic simile, as practiced especially by Homer, Virgil, and Spenser. The similes are long, and are based at times on legends or history or science. Sometimes one simile will lead into another. The result is a sense of ornateness, completeness, and scholarly thoroughness.

11. The wealth of allusion. All of human knowledge seems to be under his range, and only readers of wide reading and learning understand Milton's allusions.

Milton's style changes in respect to the particular result he wishes to achieve. His style is "Miltonic," when it is ornate, highly pictorial, steeped in imagery, and allusiveness; and it is "Miltonic" also when it is direct, plain, and straightforward, coming to the point at once. He uses the first kind, the ornate, shall we say, when he is concerned with the projection of his intense imagination, visual and auditory. The latter style, the direct one, is used usually when he is interpreting the philosophical or ethical ideas that are such an important part of his poetry. In *Paradise Lost* both styles predominate, one in the description in Book I of Satan on the lake, or the picture of Eden; the other in the debates in Hell and Heaven, and in the soliloquies of Adam or even Satan. The sonnets, particularly, employ the direct, closely-packed style. When all is said and done, it is still difficult in words to convey the essentials that make up Milton's style. It is something that must be felt, particularly heard. It is a grand experience, and one of the mountain peaks of English literary study.

PARADISE REGAINED

A. Genesis and Sources

According to the testimony of Edward Phillips, Milton had worked on the sequel to *Paradise Lost* from 1667 to 1671. Thomas Ellwood is said to have suggested the poem when he said to Milton, "Thou hast said much of *Paradise Lost,* but what hast thou to say of Paradise found?" Milton is said to have shown Ellwood the completed poem and to have credited him with putting the idea into his head. However, the theme of *Paradise Regained* is implicit in *Paradise Lost,* in its emphasis on Christ's sacrifice and the salvation of man. That Milton preferred to write of the temptation rather than of the crucifixion of Christ attests to his profound interest in ethical conflict and moral forces.

·The chief source of the poem is, of course, the Bible itself, the Gospel of Luke in the New Testament. There the three temptations given in Luke are described in similar order by Milton. Although all the more elaborate details and additions of the poem are basically Milton's own, Spenser was probably a major influence in respect to the temptation episode in Book II of the Faerie Queene, the temptation of Sir Quion, when the latter is offered wealth and power by Mammon. A greater influence than Spenser was Giles Fletcher, who in his *Christ's Victory and Triumph,* dealt with the temptation of Christ proper, and Milton could not help being inspired by it in one way or another. In its structure, *Paradise Regained* is reminiscent of the *Book of Job,* a literary triumph, according to Milton, of the epic in brief form. Just as there are the trials of Job, so Christ has his. Both works contain much dialogue, connected by brief passages at the beginning and end. Although in *Paradise Regained* allusion to classical mythology and echoes of ancient myths are almost completely absent, Milton has still made use of his learning. The fruits of his study of classical civilization and Hebrew culture and religion are evident here in abundance. There are historical and philosophical analyses, and a fine understanding of political events, laws, and customs.

B. Outline of Paradise Regained

BOOK I

The first book begins with a reference to the theme of *Paradise Lost.* Whereas, in that poem, Adam and Eve fell victims to Satan, so here, in this new epic, Satan will fall victim to the superior wisdom and courage of Christ. As usual, there is an invocation, this time to the divine spirit. When Satan hears of God's pronouncement that Christ is His "beloved Son," he appoints another council and is again selected to attempt the seduction. God, knowing what will transpire, tells the angelic host that this time there will be no failure; Christ will succeed where Adam had failed. The angels, in jubilation, sing triumphant psalms. Christ, to prepare for the temptation, departs for the wilderness and, in self-meditation, reminisces of the early years of His life, up to His present position. As yet He does not understand what was God's aim in sending Him into the wilderness. For forty days, Christ communes with His soul, until, at last Satan comes to him, disguised as an old Man, and here follows the first great temptation. Satan knows how hungry Christ is from severe fasting in the desert, and he tells Him to command the stone to be turned into bread, if He "be the Son of God." The proposal was an attack on Christ's faith, but Christ is adamant, relying on His trust in God to spare Him when the time comes. He recognizes the old man as the incarnation of evil, as Eve in the garden did not; His action is also the opposite of Eve's. Christ's obedience to God daunts Satan, and, vanquished, he vanishes as night approaches. This book is a bare recital of events, following closely the Scriptures; and Milton uses extremely plain language, which nevertheless carries with it the proper dignity and awe.

BOOK II

Christ's friends, Simon and Andrew among them, do not know what to make of his disappearance. They hope, however, that God will fulfill the promises He made concerning Christ's future. Christ's mother, Mary, although sorely grieved, patiently and obediently accepts the fact of her son's loss. Meanwhile Satan, already bested once, holds a council in mid air. He tells his followers, in a speech far less defiant and enthusiastic than those in *Paradise Lost,* that Christ is not to be easily overcome. Belial, sensual as always, proposes women as a bait, but Satan realizes that the Son of God is too much above such simple enticements. Instead, he proposes goals of higher worth, like glory, honor, and great popularity. Now we are ready for the second temptation, "the kingdoms of the world and the glory of them."

Satan knows that he must first present Christ with luxury that feeds His basic needs. He spreads before Him a gorgeous Roman banquet, not merely as a satisfaction of His gnawing hunger, but also as an exposition of the civilized refinements of ancient culture. Christ had had a dream, even before He sees the banquet of food and nourishment. Although Christ would eat, if He knew that he who gave the food was good, He rejects an offer provided by Satan himself. It is another defeat for Satan; for Christ it is a victory of temperance and restraint. The next allurement is one of riches as a means to obtaining power. Riches is for Christ, however, of no value, if it comes unaccompanied by virtue. Wealth is the "toil of fools." Wealth may purchase a kingdom, but he only is a true king that is sovereign of his own mind and body.

BOOK III

Satan, nothing daunted, proceeds to tempt Christ further. This time, he proposes glory, an even higher goal — glory that is the result of great empire. This offering elicits from Christ an impressive outburst that analyzes the real meaning of "glory." Glory is what the rabble gives, the rabble that praise vulgar things, "scarce worth the praise." He deprecates the glory or fame of military conquerors; true fame belongs to spiritual leaders and heroes who never actually sought it. This passage is reminiscent of the lines on fame in Lycidas. Now that Satan's offer of glory has been rejected, he feels that he must be more concrete and insidious in his appeals. Christ, he believes, is to undertake the great Mission, already spoken of, and, for the best accomplishment of his mission, it would be advantageous to be well armed. He shows Him some of the kingdoms of the earth, first Parthia, a kingdom of military power, which he promises to him, so that he can rule over the rest of the world. Arms is an argument of weakness, not strength, is Christ's answer; arms are vanity. His weapons are to be spiritual weapons, but not yet is the hour.

BOOK IV

Satan is now desperate; he had only a few more cards to play. He shows his intended victim the grandeur of Rome, which, in all its magnificence, he will present to Him. But Christ repels the offer with the same arguments as before. Imperial Rome's grandeur is not real grandeur; besides, it is fleeting. Satan is still more desperate. He vainly repeats that he will give all that he has proposed, if Christ will fall down and worship him. Christ, then, has rejected all kinds of enticements that have ensnared the majority of men. Christ is above things like power, dominance, sensuality, and the like. Yet one more enticement remains, which Satan hopes He will accept. This kind of glory is the glory of wisdom, of art; culture, science, all intellectual glory is represented by ancient Greece, with Athens its centre. Here Milton rises to great poetic and scholarly heights in his condensation of the achievements of Grecian literature and philosophy with its epics, lyrics, tragedies, philosophies, and oratorical masterpieces. Surely this kind of glory will be more appealing to a serious, virtuous mind such as Christ's, for surely these things are not in direct conflict with Christ's spiritual goals. Christ praises all these virtues, but rejects them, finally, preferring above these, the culture and literature of the Hebrews, of the Bible, who, in spiritual matters at least, were superior to the Pagan heresies. Real truth is not to be found in Plato or Aristotle; it can be found only in God's words, as expressed by the Hebrews or the Bible.

Now that a second temptation has failed, Satan proceeds with the last. This temptation is less intellectual or sensual than the others, but it is more dramatic. Since all else has failed, Satan will use violence, a resort used by all men who have failed to convince by reason and argument. He carries Christ to the top of the temple, and enjoins Him to stand upright at the pinnacle, if he can, or dares. Satan expects Him to fall down; instead a miracle ensues, and He remains standing. Satan, instead, is the one who falls. Angels carry Christ to a valley and feed Him, as the angels sing in triumph at the deliverance of the Lord. Later Christ goes back to His home, where He is received with more rejoicing.

C. Critical Estimate of Paradise Regained

Paradise Regained suffers in comparison with *Paradise Lost,* but it is, nevertheless, a great work, replete with the art and learning that Milton possesses. The story is told directly and symmetrically, with a steady progression towards the final defeat of Satan. The poem is mainly didactic, full of expositions of ideas, morals, spiritual struggles. Yet there intervene narrative and descriptive passages also. The speeches are closely packed with thought and learning. Instead of the ornate coloring of *Paradise Lost* we have here straightforward maturity of thought, reduced to its very essence. Especially memorable is the resumé of Pagan and Hebrew culture, and, for sensuous beauty of description, the banquet scene is also noteworthy. Milton's style, for the most part, remains dignified in its preciseness and its bareness. The poem is one of high serenity and, if it lacks great dramatic power, the subject matter is to blame, for the theme is one of intellectual and spiritual debate. Didactic poetry is not meant to be highly dramatic.

In characterization, there is a great falling off, as demanded by the subject or theme. Satan here is not the wonderful creature of *Paradise Lost;* he is desperate, aware of possible defeat, and he has little of his earlier energetic personality. He is even crude and bungling, and does not elicit our admiration, as he did in the earlier epic. Christ is a formal, stiff portrait; He is always, by nature, right and good, serene and divinely wrought. In the description of His early years, there is a tender pathos and touching solicitude. Christ, however, is a symbol of the reason, and His life is a symbol of real truth. He understands everything, and never wavers in his decisions. As a result, it is difficult to be aware of the real existence as a personality of such a figure. All that must be as it is, undoubtedly, for the nature of the theme and the protagonists demands it. Milton has illuminated the passages in the Bible that deal with his subject. He has clothed his story in dignified, beautiful verse. *Paradise Regained,* for some is the poet's greatest work.

SAMSON AGONISTES

GENERAL REVIEW

The following is a review by Professor Masson.

How came Milton to select such a subject as that of *Samson Agonistes* for one of his latest poems, if not the very latest? The reason is not far to seek. The capabilities of the theme, perceived by him through mere poetic tact as early as 1640-41, had been brought home to him with singular force and intimacy, by the experience of his own subsequent life. The story of Samson must have seemed to Milton a metaphor or allegory of much of his own life in its later stages. He also, in his veteran days, after the Restoration, was a champion at bay, a prophet-warrior left alone among men of a different faith and different manners — Philistines, who exulted in the ruin of his cause, and wreaked their wrath upon him for his past service to that cause by insults, calumnies, and jeers at his misfortunes and the cause itself. He also was blind, as Samson had been — groping about among the malignant conditions that had befallen him, helplessly dependent on the guiding of others, and bereft of the external consolations and means of resistance to his scorners that might have come to him through sight. He also had to live mainly on the imagery of the past. In that past, too, there were similarities in his case to that of Samson. Like Samson, substantially, he had been a Nazarite — no drinker of wine or strong drink, but who had always been an ascetic in his dedicated service to great designs. And the chief blunder in his life, that which had gone nearest to wreck it, and had left the most marring consequences and the most painful reflections, was the very blunder with which, twice repeated, Samson had to accuse himself. Like Samson, he had married a Philistine woman — one not of his own tribe, and having no thoughts or interest in common with his own; and, like Samson, he had suffered indignities from his wife and her relations, till he had learnt to rue the match. The consequences of Milton's unhappy first marriage (1643) in his temper and opinions form a marked train in his biography, extending far beyond their apparent end in the publication of his Divorce Pamphlets, followed by his hasty reconciliation with his wife after her two years' desertion of him (1645). Although, from that time, he lived with his first wife, without further audible complaint, till her death about 1652, and although his two subsequent marriages were happier, the recollection of his first marriage (and it was only the wife of the first marriage that he had ever seen) seems always to have been a sore in Milton's mind, and to have affected his thoughts of the marriage institution itself, and of the ways and character of women. In this respect also he could find coincidences between his own life and that of Samson, which recommended the story of Samson with far more poignancy to him in his later life than when he first looked at it in the inexperience of his early manhood. In short, there must have rushed upon Milton, contemplating in his later life the story of the blind Samson among the Philistines, so many similarities with his own case, that there is little wonder that he then selected this subject for poetic treatment.

In writing *Samson Agonistes,* Milton was executing a purpose which he had long entertained — the composition of a sacred drama.

It is commonly supposed that the *Samson* was the last of Milton's poetical works. The poem was published in 1671, in the same volume with *Paradise Regained.* The title-page bears the words "*Paradise Regained,* to which is added *Samson Agonistes*". The licenser's permission to print bears the date of July, 1670. Hayley conjectured that it was written immediately after the execution of Sir Harry Vane (June 14th, 1662). The fate of this distinguished man, for whom Milton expresses the highest admiration in one of his sonnets, and of others who had been associated with him in the affairs of the Commonwealth, the indignities shown to the remains of those who had died before the Restoration, and the general depression of the party to which all the poet's sympathies were given, may very well be alluded to in the passage beginning, "Nor only dost degrade them" (687-704). There is not wanting in these lines a reference to the writer's personal sufferings, but it is such as may have been written at any time during the later years of his life. Earlier in the drama, however, we find a passage where Samson deplores the *helplessness* of the blind, in which the reference is more definite. The litigation which took place after Milton's death with regard to his will revealed the fact that his home, after the death of his second wife (this took place in 1658), had not been a happy one. A servant gave evidence that her late master had complained to her that his daughters had "combined to defraud him in the economy of his house, and had sold some of his books in the basest manner". It is not necessary to discuss the plea which has been advanced on their behalf, and which led Dr. Johnson to pronounce that "Milton's character in his domestic relations was harsh and arbitrary". It is sufficient for our purpose to know that the poet believed himself to have been grossly wronged, and to see that this sense of injury could not have been more pointedly expressed than in the passage referred to. But this domestic unhappiness came to an end in 1665, when Milton married his third wife, from whom he seems to have received all the kindness and help which his condition demanded. There are other passages besides those cited in which we may see a reference to private or public wrongs about which the poet was feeling bitterly at the time of writing. Such are 241-276, 566-672, 749-765, where the poet seems to recall the conduct of his first wife — a recollection which would naturally be revived by the undutiful conduct of her daughters, 885-886, 1010-1060, etc. It is easy to see why the publication of a poem in which there was so much bitterness of feeling so plainly expressed should have been delayed. The wonder is that it should ever have passed the licenser's hands. But ten years had made the dominant party feel assured of their position.

POETICAL QUALITIES

It is the severe simplicity of *Samson Agonistes* which distinguishes it from Milton's other works. In this he followed with singular success the great Greek models of tragedy. Generally his style is ornate; there are passages in *Paradise Lost* which, for the profuse wealth of imagery and allusion that is lavished upon them, it would be impossible to match in this, or indeed, in any language. Here and there in the *Samson* we find a line which reminds us of the gorgeous diction which the poet knew on occasion how to employ, but the tendency is never indulged. We see it for a moment in Harapha's

> "Men call me Harapha, of stock renowned
> As Og, or Anak, and the Emims old
> That Kiriathaim held".

In Dalila's

> "I shall be named among the famousest
> Of women, sung at solemn festivals,
> Living and dead recorded", etc.

And in Manoa's final elegy over his son; but it is never allowed to pass beyond the bounds of dramatic simplicity and brevity.

To the casual reader the verse will often seem somewhat harsh and irregular. The key to its difficulties and apparent anomalies is probably to be found in the following passages, quoted from Sir Egerton Brydges and Mr. Keightley respectively:—

I believe that Milton's principle was to introduce into his lines every variety of metrical foot which is to be found in the Latin poetry, especially in the lyrics of Horace — such as not merely iambic, but spondee, dactyl, trochee, anapest, etc., and that whoever reads his lines as if they were prose, and accents them as the sense would dictate, will find that they fall into one, or rather several, of these feet, often ending, like the Latin, with a half-foot; wherever they do not, I doubt not that it arises from a different mode of accenting some word from that which was the usage in Milton's time. If there is any attempt to read Milton's verses as iambics, with a mere occasional variation of the trochee and the spondee, they will often sound very tame, instead of being, as they really are, magnificently harmonious.

In the defence thus put forward by Sir Egerton Brydges there is doubtless some truth, but it is obviously too comprehensive. No ear could appreciate the melody of verse in which a poet arbitrarily employed "every variety of metrical foot which is to be found in Latin poetry". Nor could Milton have thought himself justified in employing a method of versification for which there is no precedent to be found. At the same time we must look for the explanation of many of his metrical, as well as of his grammatical, peculiarities in his strongly pronounced classical tastes.

Mr. Keightley writes thus, in an essay which the student should, if possible, consult.

For our own part, we freely own that we are so convinced that a poet of Milton's order could not write inharmoniously, that whenever we seem to detect a want of melody we feel quite convinced that the fault must be in ourselves; and on further consideration we have always found it to be the case.

We will now examine the lines of the lyric parts which seem most likely to have offended the ear of those critics; premising, in opposition to Hallam, that he uses no "number of syllables not recognized in the usage of English poetry," for his lines are all of from two to thirty feet — all measures in use. We have shown above that in lines of three and four feet the first foot may be monosyllabic. . . . We will further observe that it seems to have been the poet's intention that the lyric parts should be read in a grave, solemn, measured tone: —

"Irrecoverably dárk, tótal eclípse" (81).
"By prívilége of deáth and búrïal" (104).
"Let us not break in upón him" (116).
"As one past hope, abandoned,
 And by himself given over" (120-121).
"That heróic, thát renówn'd,
 Irresístible Sámson? whom, unármed" (125-126).
"Chalybean tempered steel and fróck of mail
 Adamantéan proof" (133-134).
"Prison wíthin prison" (153).
"But the heárt of the fool" (298).
"O that torment shoúld not be confíned" (606).

The student will be able to apply Mr. Keightley's method for himself to any lines that may seem to fail in harmony on first reading. If he also remembers that *Samson* is a drama, and that the poet, though not intending it for performance, follows the usual dramatic rule in allowing for a slower or more rapid delivery, according to the sense of the passage, he will not find the versification presents any serious difficulties.

THE GREEK TYPE OF DRAMA AND FUNCTION OF THE CHORUS

Samson Agonistes is written on the model of the classical Greek tragedy, and in his Epistle Milton points to Æschylus, Sophocles and Euripides as being the "best rule" to all who endeavour to write Tragedy.

As such it contains a Chorus of dancers, which sings. lyric odes ("stasima") between the scenes or "episodes" of the play; these odes serve to divide the piece into what would correspond to Acts in modern drama.

The Greek stage was diminutive, and did not lend itself towards "crowd-scenes"; for the same reason bloodshed and scenes of violence are seldom or never enacted, they are usually narrated by a messenger. In *Samson* it is a messenger who reports the fate that overtakes the Philistines.

In the Greek theatre the Chorus stood grouped in the "orchestra" just below the actual stage; the play began with a "prologue", or scene before the entrance of the Chorus; then the Chorus entered with the ode styled the "parados", and remained on the stage until the end of the play.

Throughout the play, Milton has carefully followed the principles and precepts of the Greek philosopher Aristotle in his *Art of Poetry*. Aristotle states that the Chorus should be a "sharer in the action"; this is interpreted by the Roman poet Horace to mean that the Chorus should help on the action "by uttering words of encouragement and friendly counsel to the good, by rebuking the passionate, by loving the virtuous, by praising justice and peace, by obedience to the law, by recommending moderation in the appetites, and by praying to the gods to comfort the miserable, and humble the proud".

This has been summed up by the German critic Schlegal when he says that the Chorus is "the Spectator idealized", *i.e.* "is the universal voice of moral sympathy, instruction, and warning".

"The *Samson Agonistes*," says Professor Jebb, in his *Growth and Influence of Greek Classical Poetry*, "has the form of a Greek drama, but its inspiration, like its subject, is far more Hebraic than Hellenic; it concerns the mysterious dealing of Jehovah with His servant; it is full of questionings and strivings like those of Job, followed by such a triumph as rings through the song of Miriam or of Deborah."

In his Introductory Epistle "Of that sort of Dramatic Poem which is called Tragedy", Milton states that division into act and scene, referring chiefly to the stage (to which this work never was intended), is here omitted.

In this edition, however, it has been thought advisable to divide the text into Acts conforming with the generally accepted structural analysis of the Poem, and it is hoped that this may prove of assistance to students to whom the structure of the Greek type of drama is not familiar.

POLITICAL ALLUSIONS

In many ways the theme of *Samson Agonistes* is a veiled presentation of that period of Milton's life when tragedy had overtaken him; he too, had fallen on "evil days and evil tongues", the past lay in ruins behind him; the present fraught with danger and difficulties, the future dark, bleak and uncertain.

It will be obvious that he is referring to his own misfortunes and suffering in the lines in which Samson soliloquises on his blindness and comments on the ingratitude and folly of his countrymen.

The Commonwealth had crashed in ruins — Samson represents Puritanism fallen and captive — and the Philistines stand for the Royalists triumphant at the Restoration.

The festivals held by the Philistines in the Temple of Dagon represent the dissolute manners prevailing at the court of Charles II.

THE STORY OF THE POEM

The play begins with Samson asking someone to guide him to a place where he may enjoy the fresh air — a change from his damp, unwholesome prison. Then he enters on a soliloquy which explains why on this day he has a brief respite from his toil. It is the feast-day of Dagon, the sea-idol of the Philistines, so that no work can be done. Instead, the people are making merry, and Samson is glad to be at some distance from the noise of mirth. While he eases his body, tired with the hard labour which he is forced to do, he thinks about his present state of captivity and calls to mind that his birth had been foretold by an angel, that he had been gifted with great strength, that he had been destined to deliver the Israelites from their enemies, the Philistines. Then he recalls how he disclosed to his wife, Dalila, the secret that his strength lay in his hair, and how, after she had betrayed him into the hands of his enemies, he had been made captive by them and deprived of the wonderful gift of sight. He dwells on the agony of being thus "blind among enemies", breaking out into the lamentation:—

> "O, dark, dark, dark, amid the blaze of noon,
> Irrecoverably dark, total eclipse,
> Without all hope of day",

and feels that he is almost "a moving grave". In the midst of his grief he hears footsteps and fears that his enemies are coming to torment him. The people who arrive, however, are his friends, the Danites, who (in the form of the Chorus) reveal their consternation at seeing the bowed figure of Samson. They contrast with this the heroic young man who had exhibited such feats of strength which "might have subdued the earth". They address him gently, pointing out that they have come to give him some comfort if that is possible, and he, while thanking them for their friendship, tells them that he has come to this abject state through his own weakness of character. While pointing out that both his first wife (from Timna) and his second, Dalila, had deceived him, and that the Israelites themselves had not been helpful in seeking to bring about their own deliverance, he still, in humility, ascribes his downfall to his own foolishness. The Chorus try to hearten him by pointing out that God's ways are just.

At the close of their speech, they call Samson's attention to the approach of his white-haired father, Manoa. When Manoa arrives, he is horrified at the change in his son, the man

> "who, single combatant,
> Duelled their armies ranked in proud array,
> Himself an army, now unequal match
> To save himself against a coward armed
> At one spear's length".

Like Samson in an earlier speech, he refers to the appearance of the angels before his son's birth, and seems inclined to blame God for subjecting one whom He Himself had thus honoured to such "foul indignities".

Samson, however, answers this reproach against the Almighty by explaining how his wives had deceived him and especially how Dalila by her importunity had at length led him to reveal to her the source of his great strength. Manoa recalls his earlier objections to Samson's marriages, and states that his son is now paying heavily for these mistakes. He explains that the cause of his greatest bitterness at that moment is the realisation that the Philistines' feast for Dagon is really being celebrated on account of their former enemy's captivity. Samson confesses that all this honour is being given to Dagon through his own fault, but refuses to believe that God will allow Dagon to be victorious; eventually the heathen god will certainly be overthrown. Manoa agrees with this and says that he has already tried to free Samson by appealing to some Philistine lords about his ransom. In spite of Samson's protestations concerning this action, he holds out the hope that the blind man may soon be able to go home and there ask God's pardon for his sins. Samson states that his main sin has been pride; he has never been intemperate, but he *has* indulged in overweening pride, and he has been weak also in his dealings with Dalila. In spite of his father's suggestion that strength is returning with the growth of his hair, he feels that his death is not far off,

> "I shall shortly be with them that rest",

and, indeed, his petition is for

> "Speedy death
> The close of all my miseries, and the balm".

His friends, the Chorus, praise him for his temperance in youth and his patience under his present trials, and they point out how often ills befall mankind, praying that Samson may have, at any rate, a peaceful end. Then they see a new arrival, "female of sex it seems", very resplendent in bright colours, and realise that this is Dalila. In spite of Samson's entreaty that she may be kept from him, she approaches her husband in apparently a contrite and tearful mood, stating that she wants to make amends for her former conduct. The excuses she puts forward are that she used to be inquisitive and unable to keep a secret, but adds that these faults are common to many women. She reproaches him for being so unwise as to trust a secret to "woman's frailty". Then she states that she was afraid he would leave her as he left his first wife, and so tried to keep him by her side by depriving him of his strength. As for revealing the secret, she was assured by the Philistines that no harm would befall him. She agrees that she has brought him to his present terrible state, but thinks he ought to pardon her because she is his wife. Samson does not become a prey to her wiles; he declares that he *had* been very wrong to trust her, but says her "weakness" was the lack of power to resist Philistine bribes, and he continues,

> "All wickedness is weakness; that plea, therefore,
> With God or man will gain thee no remission".

As for the plea of wifehood and love, he puts that aside with contempt. Then she declares that the Philistines had cajoled her into giving them the secret because they were her "own" people and

> "to the public good
> Private respects must yield".

But Samson is satirical about this plea, too, and man and wife fall into dispute about the comparative merits of their former arguments. Even when Dalila promises to take him home and nurse him in his affliction, Samson's anger does not abate; he orders her to go before he does her any bodily harm, and says, "At distance I forgive thee; go with that". Then Dalila gibes at him, pointing out that she will humble herself no longer, but will enjoy among the Philistines the great fame of having delivered him into their hands.

The Danites realise that Samson has been very firm not to forgive her speedily, and declare that such firmness is necessary in a husband. They then remark that Samson is to have another visitor, for the giant Harapha is approaching, looking exceedingly defiant, though he is not clad as if for a fight. Harapha soon makes known his reason for coming; he merely wants to see the hero whom he has never met in combat. Samson suggests that the best way to know him is not merely to look at his limbs, but to taste his strength, and this remark brings a boastful speech from Harapha, who says that he obviously cannot fight with a blind man, but if they *had* met previously *he* would certainly have been the victor. Samson offers to fight him with only an oaken staff, and urges the other to equip himself with glittering armour, a spear and a shield, saying that he would put his trust in God, Who is stronger than Dagon. In spite of his taunt,

> "Fair honour that thou dost thy God, in trusting
> He will accept thee to defend His cause,
> A murderer, a revolter and a robber",

and his declaration,

> "To fight with thee no man of arms will deign",

Harapha speedily goes away when Samson explains that though his heels are "fettered", his fist is "free", and threatens to attack him,

> "And with one buffet lay thy structure low,
> Or swing thee in the air, then dash thee down
> To the hazard of thy brains and shattered sides".

The Chorus notice that the giant is somewhat crestfallen in his retreat, but fear that he will stir up the lords to afflict Samson further. This, however, does not worry Samson, and he does not even seem troubled when an officer appears stating that the Philistines demand from him some feats of strength to celebrate the feast of Dagon. He at first refuses firmly to suffer this indignity, saying in response to the demand that he must be led to the temple, "I will not come", and after the officer's departure, he expresses to the Chorus his determination not to use the consecrated gift of strength which he feels returning to him by honouring a heathen god. However, by the time the officer returns with a more peremptory message, he has come to the decision to accompany him.

The two have scarcely set off for the temple, the officer praising Samson's decision and Samson assuring the Chorus that he will perform no unworthy action, when Manoa arrives. He is in good heart, for he thinks that he will be successful in securing his son's freedom by paying a ransom. The Chorus rejoice with him, but their manifestations of pleasure are cut short by a dreadful cry, a "hideous noise", very different from the earlier sounds of amazement and hilarity. This cry appears to come from the lips of people smitten by disaster. Manoa and his friends, awestruck, decide to wait for news. Soon a messenger arrives bringing the tidings that Samson, after showing several feats of strength, had asked permission to rest himself by leaning on the two massive pillars that supported the roof. When led between these, he had declared that he would amaze the large assembled company, and he had then uprooted the pillars so that the roof fell and all in the building had perished.

The play ends with lamentation and adulation from the Chorus, after Manoa's noble words:—

> "Nothing is here for tears, nothing to wail
> Or knock the breast; no weakness, no contempt,
> Dispraise or blame; nothing but well and fair,
> And what may quiet us in a death so noble".

CHARACTERS IN THE POEM

SAMSON

When Samson first appears, he arouses sympathy for his hopeless condition. He is dejected and wonders why he was ever chosen by God to be a leader, and why his birth was foretold by angels if he is made "the scorn and gaze" of his enemies,

> "To grind in brazen fetters under task
> With this heaven-gifted strength".

But even here he feels that though he is "Eyeless, in Gaza, at the mill, with slaves", he must not blame God for his situation, since that has really been brought about by his own weakness. It is this *weakness* that he stresses the whole time; in his talk with his father he explains how he first allowed the woman Timna to learn a secret from him and then how, when tired by Dalila's importunity, he actually told her his "capital secret" — "I yielded and unlocked her all my heart". Anyone "with a grain of manhood", he argues, would have withstood Dalila's wiles, but "foul effeminacy" made him "her bond-slave".

Later he declared, in answer to Dalila's plea of being merely a "weak" woman, "All wickedness is weakness".

His *dejection* is made apparent by his own words and by the effect of the sight of him on other people. More than anything else the loss of eyesight afflicts him:—

> "O dark, dark, dark, amid the blaze of noon,
> Irrecoverably dark, total eclipse,
> Without all hope of day!" (l. 80 *ff*).

He feels that to be "blind among enemies" is an overwhelming sorrow, yet the shame of having betrayed his people is greater than any physical affliction. He tells the Chorus,

> "Yet that which was the worst now least afflicts me,
> Blindness; for, had I sight, confused with shame,
> How could I once look up?" (l. 195 *ff*).

He realises that this dejection is sapping his strength, but seems quite reconciled to the drooping of his "genial spirits", and feels that since "the race of glory" is run, his "race of shame" will soon be finished too,

"And I shall shortly be with them that rest" (l. 598).

His attitude is obviously one of great physical and mental weariness, for the members of the Chorus say,

> "See how he lies at random, carelessly diffused,
> With languished head unpropped,
> As one past hope, abandoned,
> And by himself given over" (ll. 118-121).

And Manoa, as well as the Chorus, remarks on the "miserable change" in the former strong and upright Israelite.

Samson is *contrite* and *quite willing to bear his punishment.* In many speeches he expresses his contrition. He declares that though Dalila tempted him, "She was not the prime cause, but I myself" (l. 234). He recognises the fairness of his punishment,

> "Servile mind,
> Rewarded well with servile punishment" (ll. 412-413),

and desires expiation—

> "let me here
> As I deserve, pay on my punishment,
> And expiate, if possible, my crime
> Shameful garrulity" (ll. 488-490).

When Dalila comes, he is willing to bear her presence as an additional punishment—

> "God sent her to debase me,
> And aggravate my folly" (ll. 999-1000).

His *patience under his trials,* due to this contrition, is such that the Chorus remark upon it:

> "Patience is more oft the exercise
> Of saints, the trial of their fortitude,
> Making them each his own deliverer,
> And victor over all
> That tyranny or fortune can inflict" (l. 1287 *ff*),

and continue,

> "sight bereaved
> May chance to number thee with those
> Whom patience finally must crown" (l. 1294 *ff*).

Samson's *trust in God* is very great. He is quite sure that Dagon will not be allowed to be victorious:—

> "Dagon must stoop, and shall ere long receive
> Such a discomfit, as shall quite despoil him
> Of all those boasted trophies won on me" (l. 468 *ff*).

He *keeps strickly the laws of the Israelites,* and declares that he will comply in nothing "Scandalous or forbidden in our law" (l. 1408).

In many ways, it is clear that Samson is very *sensible.* He realises that the Israelites themselves really threw away the advantages he had at one time procured for them:—

> "Had Judah that day joined, or one whole tribe,
> They had by this possessed the towers of Gath,
> And lorded over them whom now they serve"
> (ll. 265-267).

He explains how he managed to evade his enemies—

> "Not flying, but forecasting in what place
> To set upon them, what advantaged best" (ll. 254-255).

He is not deluded by Dalila's arguments, but takes these point by point and shows their fallacy, declaring that neither weakness nor love could excuse her crime, and that her excuse

> "that to the public good
> Private respects must yield" (ll. 867-868),

is founded only on her own hypocrisy.

He argues that since, when he was strong, she could "sell" him, she is much more likely to do so now that he is

> "Helpless, thence easily contemned and scorned
> And last neglected?" (ll. 943-944).

He shows craft as well as courage in the method he employs to bring ruin on his foes:—

> "he his guide requested . . .
> As over-tired, to let him lean a while
> With both his arms on those two massy pillars,
> That to the archèd roof gave main support" (l. 1630 *ff*).

He was certainly very *courageous;* in his interview with Harapha, he shows this in every speech. He begins by remarking, "The way to know were not to see, but taste" (l. 1091), and drives the giant away by the threat, "My heels are fettered, but my fist is free". He is ready to meet a foe in argument or in physical strength. His father declares that before his blindness, Samson,

> "single combatant,
> Duelled their armies ranked in proud array,
> Himself an army" (ll. 344-346,)

and the Chorus bear out these words by their tribute,

> "In seeking just occasion to provoke
> The Philistine, thy country's enemy,
> Thou never wast amiss" (ll. 237-240).

Samson himself, while not boasting, gives an account of some of his exploits, stating, "The deeds themselves, though mute, spoke loud the doer" (l. 248).

His *humility* is evident from his willingness to take his punishment—

> "Nothing of all these evils hath befallen me
> But justly" (ll. 374-375),

but he himself says that in earlier days he was "swollen with pride" (l. 530), and he determines to go with the officer,

> "Because they shall not trail me through their streets
> Like a wild beast" (ll. 1402-1403),

showing that there is pride still in his disposition.

He is *honourable,* declaring that he will do nothing "that may dishonour our law, or stain my vow of Nazarite" (ll. 1385-1386), and that the work he does for the Philistines is but

> "labour,
> Honest and lawful, to deserve my food
> Of those who have me in their civil power" (l. 1365 *ff*).

He possesses *determination,* for he withstood Dalila's wiles for a considerable time, and is very definite in his reply to the officer, "I will not come" (l. 1332).

He can be *ironical,* as in his conversation with Harapha when he ejaculates, "My nation was subjected to your lords!" (l. 1205), with Dalila when he sneeringly remarks,

> "But zeal moved thee;
> To please thy gods thou didst it" (ll. 895-896);

and again in connection with a woman's being worsted in argument.

"For want of words no doubt, or lack of breath!
Witness when I was worried with thy peals" (ll. 905-906).

Dalila seems to bring out the worst traits in Samson, but even so, he gives her a grudging pardon — "At distance I forgive thee; go with that" (l. 954).

He is *grateful* to the Chorus for their friendship and to Manoa for his kindness; he shows a great *love of liberty,* and thinks nothing more corrupt than "to love bondage more than liberty" (l. 270); he is *abstemious,* and drinks only from "fountain or fresh current"; he is *dignified,* as is made evident by the messenger's account of his last moments; and, finally, he is so *noble* that we feel the only fitting words for his epitaph are those of his father—

"Samson hath quit himself
Like Samson, and heroicly hath finished
A life heroic".

MANOA

Two outstanding characteristics of Manoa are his *kindliness* and his *optimism.* He is evidently old, as the Chorus speaks of him as "reverend sire", and describe his "careful step" and his "locks white as down". He shows great kindness towards his son, while in no way condoning his fault. In his love for Samson he is inclined to grumble at God.

"Methinks whom God has chosen once
To worthiest deeds, if he through frailty err,
He should not so o'erwhelm, and as a thrall
Subject him to so foul indignities,
Be it but for honour's sake of former deeds" (l. 368 *ff*).

His kindness is shown particularly in his *generosity,* for he is so good to Samson that he spares no effort to get him ransomed. He tells his son at their first meeting,

"I already have made way
To some Philistian lords, with whom to treat
About thy ransom" (ll. 481-483),

and later explains to the Chorus how he has made contact with three types of the Philistian nobles, those who were harsh, those who were indifferent to suffering but not averse to gain, and those who really had some gentle feelings. He tells his friends that he will gladly give any amount of money to free Samson:—

> "His ransom, if my whole inheritance
> May compass it, shall willingly be paid
> And numbered down; much rather I shall choose
> To live the poorest in my tribe, than richest,
> And he in that calamitous prison left.
> No, I am fixed not to part hence without him.
> For his redemption, all my patrimony,
> If need be, I am ready to forgo
> And quit; not wanting him, I shall want nothing
>
> (l. 1476 *ff*).

Further, he states how he will care for Samson — "It shall be my delight to tend his eyes" (l. 1400).

His *perseverance,* too, is shown in the way he struggles to get the Philistian lords to agree to a ransom. He has the Israelites' *love for home,* and calls Samson's attention to the ill that has befallen "thy father's house" (l. 445).

He is very *sensible* in his advice to Samson when he is dejected.

> "Be penitent, and for thy fault contrite,
> But act now in thy own affliction, son,
> Repent the sin, but if the punishment
> Thou canst avoid, self-preservation bids" (ll. 502-505).

In the same speech, he shows his good sense in not being foolishly sympathetic towards his son's feeling that death is preferable to further living. He remarks that self-abasement can be carried too far, and can even become a sort of inverted pride—

> "Which argues over-just, and self-displeased
> For self-offence, more than for God offended"
>
> (ll. 514-515).

His *optimism* is very great; indeed, on some occasions it seems excessive. He thinks that Samson may be forgiven for his sin:—

> "Perhaps
> God will relent, and quit thee all His debt" (ll. 508-509),

and even thinks the clemency of the Almighty is so great that,

> "God will restore him eyesight to his strength" (l. 1503).

He is very *courageous,* and when the messenger is unwilling to break the sad news of Samson's death he urges him to speak, saying,

> "Suspense in news is torture; speak them out" (l. 1569).

To him is given the calm courage which renders him able in the midst of his deep grief to say of his dead son,

> "Nothing is here for tears, nothing to wail
> Or knock the breast; no weakness, no contempt,
> Dispraise, or blame; nothing but well and fair,
> And what may quiet us in a death so noble"
>
> (ll. 1721-1724).

DALILA

We first hear of Dalila from Samson himself, and his description of her is not flattering; he calls her, "That specious monster, my accomplished snare" (l. 230).

She is obviously very *fond of dress,* for the Chorus speaks of her as "bedecked, ornate and gay", and her gait is assured; she walks "like a stately ship".

She appears *hypocritical,* for though she can taunt Samson and, at the end, even flout him she arrives "with head declined", and, "Like a fair flower surcharged with dew, she weeps" (l. 728). She states that she will intercede to the lords for his release and that she will tend him "to old age".

Samson is not beguiled by her; he remarks on her *cunning,* exclaiming, "Malice not repentance brought thee hither" (l. 821). She is very *plausible* in making excuses, declaring that she wanted to learn his secrets in order to keep his love for herself alone, and that she revealed them in order to prevent his entering upon perilous enterprises; she thought, when captured, he would be, "Mine and love's prisoner, not the Philistines'" (l. 808).

When she cannot convince Samson either by *her appeal to his chivalry*—

> "love hath oft, well meaning, wrought much woe,
> Yet always pity or pardon hath obtained" (ll. 813-814),

or by her *untruthfulness*—

> "Hear what assaults I had, what snares besides,
> What sieges girt me round, ere I consented" (ll. 845-846),

she becomes *taunting* and declares that she will

> "be named among the famousest
> of women, sung at solemn festivals" (ll. 982-983).

That her verbal wiles were able to deceive her listeners is obvious
from the remark of the Chorus:—

> "She's gone, a manifest serpent by her sting
> Discovered in the end, till now concealed" (ll. 997-998).

HARAPHA

In his relationship to Samson, Harapha shows himself to be a
mocker and a *coward*. He is also exceedingly *boastful* and *rude*. His
rudeness is especially shown in his remark, "And thou hast need
much washing to be touched" (l. 1107), but it is latent in all his
taunts, such as,

> "I thought
> Gyves and the mill had tamed thee" (ll. 1092-1093).

He boasts loudly—

> "I should have forced thee soon with other arms,
> Or left thy carcass where the ass lay thrown"
> (ll. 1096-1097),

wishing that "fortune" had brought him into contact with Samson
when he "Wrought such wonders with an ass's jaw" (l. 1095). But
when Samson offers battle with him, declaring "My heels are fettered,
but my fist is free" (l. 1235), he soon turns away, "Stalking with less
unconscionable strides" (l. 1245) than on his first appearance.

THE CHORUS

The chorus is composed of friends of Samson, Danites like himself.
The members take a definite part in the action, comforting Samson,
telling him who is coming and discussing with him the characters of
his visitors. They carry on a dialogue with Manoa and show their
sympathy with his joys and sorrows. When he is optimistic about the
ransom, the friendliness of the Chorus is shown in the words,

> "Thy hopes are not ill founded nor seem vain
> Of his delivery, and thy joy thereon
> Conceived, agreeable to a father's love,
> In both which we, as next, participate" (l. 1504 *ff*).

They hearten Samson as he goes to his ordeal:

> "Go, and the Holy One
> Of Israel by thy guide" (ll. 1427-1428).

They are *knowledgeable* and *helpful* in recommending patience by
such words as,

> "Many are the sayings of the wise
> In ancient and in modern books enrolled,
> Extolling patience as the truest fortitude" (ll. 652-654),

and

> "But patience is more oft the exercise
> Of saints, the trial of their fortitude,
> Making them each his own deliverer,
> And victor over all
> That tyranny or fortune can inflict" (l. 1287 *ff*).

They have the last word, and it is of profound wisdom:—

> "All is best, though we oft doubt
> What the unsearchable dispose
> Of Highest Wisdom brings about,
> And ever best found in the close" (l. 1745 *ff*).

NOTES

Agonistes. One who contends as an athlete in public games, a wrestler.

THE ARGUMENT

equals, persons of his own age.

Manoa. A native of Zorah, of the tribe of Dan. See *Judges,* xiii, 2-25.

Philistines. It is probable that they were originally Aryan pirates who forced a settlement for themselves among the Semitic tribes of the Mediterranean.

catastrophe. The event which brings about the climax of the play.

PROLOGUE — Lines 1-175

1. **lend thy guiding hand.** Addressed to the guide by whom he is led.
5. **servile toil,** toiling like a slave, the task of grinding corn.
9. **Unwholesome draught,** *i.e.* unhealthy to breathe.
11. **day-spring,** the dawn.
13. **Dagon, their sea-idol.** The famous god of the Philistines, represented as half man and half fish.
20. **hornets armed.** Represented as the scourge of God.
24. **Twice by an Angel.** See *Judges,* xiii, 3 and 9.
27. **charioting,** removing as in a chariot.
31. **separate to God,** set apart for God. See *Judges,* xiii, 3-5.
35. **under task,** in forced labour.
37. **labour of a beast,** *i.e.* work fit for asses.
39. **Promise . . . deliverer.** See *Judges,* xiii, 5.
41. **Eyeless . . . slaves.** This line vividly sums up the climax of the sorrows of the captive Samson. It was from the fortified town of Gaza that Samson carried away the town gates (see *Judges,* xvi, 3); it was here that Dalila enticed him to his doom.
57. **subserve,** serve in a subordinate capacity.
70. **prime first,** See *Genesis,* i, 3.
75. **dark in light,** blind in the midst of light. A juxtaposition of words used in an apparently contradictory sense.

75-79. In these lines Milton appears to paint a portrait of himself.

83. **O first created beam.** *Cf.* the apostrophe to light, *Paradise Lost*, iii, 1-12. **thou great Word.** See *Genesis*, i, 3.

87. **silent as the moon.** *Luna silens,* "silent moon", was a Latin phrase for absence of moonlight.

89. **Hid in her vacant interlunar cave,** *i.e.* when there is no moon, between the old and the new moon.

118. **at random,** negligently.

121. **over,** up.

122. **slavish . . . O'er-worn,** the dress of a slave, ill-fitting clothes, worn out.

128-131. **Who tore . . . ridiculous.** See *Judges,* xiv, 5-6, and xv, 15.

133. **Chalybean-tempered.** Such as would be made by the Chalybes, represented as dwelling on the southern shore of the Black Sea, and famous among the ancients for working iron and steel.

134. **adamantean proof,** impenetrable armour.

136. **insupportably,** not to be resisted.

138. **bold Ascalonite,** *i.e.* Philistines of Ascalon, one of their five chief cities. See note l. 981.

145. **In Ramath-lechi.** "He cast away the jawbone out of his hand, and called that place Ramath-lehi." See *Judges,* xv, 17.

147. **Azza.** Another form of Gaza.

148. **Hebron, seat of giants.** Hebron was the city of Arba, the father of Anak, and the children of Anak were giants. See *Joshua,* xv, 13 *Numbers,* xiii, 33.

149. **No journey of a Sabbath-day.** The Jews were forbidden to go long journeys on the Sabbath-day.

150. **Like whom,** like him whom, *i.e.* like the giant Atlas, whom Grecian mythology fabled to bear up heaven.

163. **visual beam,** light to see by.

172. **the sphere of fortune.** The well-known metaphor of the "wheel of fortune".

FIRST EPISODE — Lines 176-292

177. **unjointed,** disjointed, inarticulate.

181. **Eshtaol and Zora's fruitful vale.** Zorah was his birthplace, and Eshtaol lay near it. See *Judges,* xiii, 25. Both of them were in a valley. See *Joshua,* xv, 33.

184. **swage,** assuage, allay, soothe.

203. **Proverbed for a fool,** made a by-word. "And now I am their song, yea, I am their by-word." (See *Job,* xxx, 9.)

207. **mean,** average.

209. **transverse,** out of my due course.

241. **That fault I take not . . .** Milton probably intended to reproach his countrymen indirectly, and as plainly as he dared, with the Restoration of Charles II, which he accounted the restoration of slavery. He pursues the same subject again in ll. 678-700.

247. **ambition.** In the literal sense, going about convassing for applause.

252. **Judea.** That part of Judea which belonged to the tribe of Judah.
253. **rock of Etham.** Within the borders of the tribe, not far from Ramath-lehi.
261. **but cords . . . flame.** This is the Bible metaphor. See *Judges,* xv, 14.
263. **A trivial weapon,** *i.e.* the ass's jawbone. See *Judges,* xv, 14-19. "Trivial" = worthless, common.
268. **But what more oft.** In this passage is probably intended a secret satire upon the English nation, which, according to Milton's republican politics, by restoring the King had chosen bondage with ease rather than strenuous liberty.
278. **how Succoth . . . Penuel.** The men of Succoth and of Penuel refused to give food to Gideon and his men when they were pursuing Zebah and Zalmunna, kings of the Midianites. See *Judges,* viii, 1-21.
281. **Madian.** Midian in the Old Testament, but Madian in *Acts,* vii, 29.
282. **how ingrateful . . . Jephtha.** Jephthah subdued the children of Ammon, and he is said to have defended Israel "by argument not worse than by his shield and spear" owing to the message he sent to the King of the Ammonites. See *Judges,* xi, 14-27.
289. **For want . . . Shibboleth.** See *Judges,* xii, 1-6.

FIRST STASIMON — Lines 293-325
297-298. The rhyme here and in ll. 303-306 gives a contemptuous effect. Notice also the irregular metre.
303. **His glory's diminution.** To diminish God's glory is high treason against Him.
305. **ravel,** get entangled, become perplexed, fall into confusion.
312. **national obstriction,** the binding force of national laws. The reference is to the Mosaic Law that forbade all true Israelites from intermarrying with Gentiles.
318. **Nazarite . . . purity.** Not a vow of celibacy, but the "national obstriction" mentioned above. A Nazarite was a priest set apart ("separate to God", l. 31). See *Judges,* xiii, 5.
321. **Unclean, unchaste.** According to Mosaic law, Dalila as a heathen was unclean; on the other hand, reason acquits her of being unclean or unchaste in any other sense.

SECOND EPISODE — Lines 326-651
333. **uncouth,** strange and unknown; a Philistine town, and so not frequented by Israelites.
335. **informed,** instructed, guided.
339. **erst,** once, formerly.
345. **Duelled,** fought in duel. It is implied that Samson was engaged in single combat, although it says that he fought their armies.
360. **graces,** favours, blessings.
364. **miracle of men,** object of men's admiration and wonder.
368. **Alas! methinks.** An allusion to the indignities offered by the Royalists to the remains of Cromwell and Ireton shortly after the Restoration.
373. **Appoint not heavenly disposition,** do not (try to) arrange heavenly dispensation.

380. **A Canaanite,** *i.e.* Gentiles as a whole. The Philistines were not Canaanites, but both were the common enemies of Israel.

382. **she of Timna.** See *Judges*, xiv.

390. **by the scent conceived.** Perhaps Milton is thinking of Danaë's conception of Perseus. While she was shut up in a dungeon Zeus visited her in a shower of gold.

403. **blandished parleys,** soothing fair speeches.

405. **over-watched,** tired out.

424. **I state not that,** I do not enter upon, give an opinion upon, that point.

442. **Disglorified,** deprived of glory.

453. **idolists.** A word coined by Milton for "idolaters".

454. **diffidence of,** distrust in.

471. **blank,** cause to turn pale.

473. **as a prophecy.** Examples are numerous in ancient literature of the belief in omens drawn, as here, from spoken words. In these words the downfall of Dagon's worshippers is prophesied, as the death of Samson is in other places.

499. **a sin . . . condemn.** Alluding to the story of Tantalus, who, in Roman mythology, was punished for revealing the secrets of the gods.

515. **For . . . offended,** *i.e.* for having offended his own sense of pride rather than for having offended God.

516. **what offered means.** "What" is here used for "those which". The expression is difficult, but to this effect: reject not these means of ransom, which, for anything one can tell, God may have set before us, or suggested to us in order to return thee to thy home.

518. **His sacred house,** *i.e.* the tabernacle.

528. **The sons of Anak.** See note l. 148.

531. **my affront,** coming face to face with me.

533. **venereal trains,** *i.e.* the devices and wiles of his wife when he lost himself to her charms.

543. **dancing ruby,** *i.e.* sparkling red wine, rubied nectar.

550. **clear milky juice.** A strange expression for pure running water. Milton had, however, in *Paradise Lost,* v, 306, termed water a milky "stream" *i.e.* as sweet as milk.

569. **robustious,** vigorous, strong, robust.

571. **craze,** break, weaken. In *Paradise Lost,* xii, 210, the word is applied to the breaking of chariot wheels.

574. **draff of servile food,** waste grain of slaves' food. *Cf.* "servile toil", note l. 5.

578. **annoy,** harass, do hurt and damage: a much stronger word than now.

581. **who caused . . . battle.** See note l. 263.

590. **All otherwise.** The student should note the sublime pathos of this speech.

600. **humorous black,** a gloomy mood. The word "melancholy" literally means "black humour", "black bile".

612. **accidents,** properties, qualities or attributes.

620. **immedicable,** incurable.

628. **Alp.** Synonymous with "high mountain".

SECOND STASIMON — Lines 652-709

657. **consolatories,** devotional books professing to offer consolation.

677. **head without name,** *i.e.* men of no repute.

678. **but such as thou.** A reference to the leaders of the Puritans.

687-696. These lines allude to the fate of the Puritan party; there can be no doubt they are intended to refer to the brutal indignities offered to the remains of the Commonwealth leaders.

700. **crude,** premature, unripe, before its time — the ordinary English sense of the word.

THIRD EPISODE — Lines 710-1009

715. **Of Tarsus.** There is frequent mention in Scripture of the ships of Tarshish, which Milton might conceive to be the same as Tarsus in Cilicia.

   the isles of Javan. Greece, since Javan or Ion, the fourth son of Japhet, is said to have peopled Greece and Ionia (a district on the west coast of Asia Minor).

716. **Gadire.** Cadiz.

717. **bravery,** finery.

719. **hold them play,** fill them out.

720. **amber scent.** Amber or ambergris was a favourite perfume in Milton's time.

748. **hyæna.** Reputed to counterfeit the voice of a man and draw shepherds out of their cottages at night, in order to kill them.

760. **With goodness principled,** grounded in the principles of goodness.

785. **parle,** parley, negotiation with a view to coming to terms.

803. **made for me,** favoured me, suited my purpose.

838. **hope,** hope for.

840. **Knowing . . . betrayed,** knowing myself to be betrayed by thee, as I must come to do.

853. **civil duty,** duty as a citizen, to the state.

857. **the priest.** The character of the priest is the poet's own addition to the Scriptural account. It is obviously a satire on the ministers of the Church.

871. **circling,** reluctant to come to the point at issue, evasive.

901. **varnished colours,** deceitful or specious excuses or appearances.

919. **abroad,** out of doors.

936. **adder's wisdom.** See *Psalm* lviii, 4-5.

945. **uxorious.** Here the meaning is "in obedience to my wife's will".

971. **Fame.** This description of Fame is mainly the invention of Milton's imagination. The "double-mouthed" and "contrary blast" are taken from Chaucer's *House of Fame*.

981. **Ecron . . . Gath.** Ashdod, Ascalon, Gath, Gaza and Ekron were the five cities of the Philistines. See *I Samuel,* vi, 16-18.

989. **Jael.** See *Judges,* iv. 4-24.

1009. **Not wedlock-treachery.** Wedlock treachery (as distinct from mere lovers' quarrels) does not end "in pleasing concord".

THIRD STASIMON — Lines 1010-1060

1012. **inherit,** possess. A frequent meaning in the Bible and in Milton.

1014. **hit,** *i.e.* hit upon the truth.

1016. **in one day,** *i.e.* it matters not whether men should sit for one day or seven trying to find it out, so difficult is it to solve.

1020. **paranymph.** Formerly a common word in early writers for the "overseer of a wedding". In the story in *Judges,* xiv, 20, it is said, "Samson's wife was given to his companion, whom he had used as his friend".

1022. **nor . . . nuptials,** nor would both (thy wives) so easily have dissolved the marriage tie.

1030. **affect,** aim at, incline towards.

1037. **thorn Intestine,** "thorn in the flesh", inward disturbance.

1039. **A cleaving mischief.** An allusion to the poisoned shirt sent to Hercules by his wife Deianeira.

1042. **dotage,** excessive fondness.

1057. **lour,** frown angrily.

FOURTH EPISODE — Lines 1061-1291

1068. **The giant Harapha of Gath.** A fictitious character, but he is appropriately introduced by Milton, and the name is not without some foundation in Scripture. Arapha, or rather Rapha, was father of the giants of the valley of Rephaim. See II Samuel, v, 18, 22. The literal meaning of Rephaim is "the giants". For "Gath", see note l. 981.

1073. **habit,** dress.

1074. **Or . . . or,** either . . . or.

   alike to me he comes, *i.e.* it makes no difference to me.

1075. **fraught,** freight, *i.e.* what he brings with him, his purpose in coming.

1080. **As Og . . . Emims old.** Og, who was of a race of giants, was the King of Bashan. See *Deuteronomy,* iii, 3. The giant Anak was the father of the Anakims (see note l. 148). Emims was a name given by the Moabites to the Anakims. See *Deuteronomy,* ii. 10-11.

1081. **That Kiriathaim held.** See *Genesis,* xiv, 5.

1087. **listed field.** The enclosed ground in which medieval tilts and combats were fought.

1091. **taste,** make trial.

1093. **Gyves,** fetters.

1095. See note l. 263.

1109. **assassinated.** Here means "taken by treachery", "craftily betrayed".

1113. **close-banded,** secretly leagued together.

1120. **brigandine.** Coat of mail, ancient armour of scale-like plates and many joints.

   habergeon. Mail protection for neck and shoulders.

1121. **Vant-brace.** Armour for the arms.

       greaves. Armour for the legs.

       gauntlet. Iron glove.

1122. **A weaver's beam.** "The staff of Goliath's spear was like a weaver's beam." See *I Samuel*, xvii, 7.

1138. **ruffled porcupines.** A recollection of Shakespeare's lines:
"And each particular hair to stand on end,
Like quills upon the fretful porpentine" (*i.e.* porcupine)
                    (*Hamlet,* I, v. 19-20).

1146. **invocate,** invoke, pray for.

1181. **tongue-doughty,** valiant with the tongue (only).

1183-1191. See *Judges,* xiv, 19, and xv, 10-13.

1195. **politician,** politic, cunning, crafty.

1218. **my known offence.** The betrayal of his secret to Dalila.

1220. **shifts refuted,** subterfuges exposed.

1222. **defies three thrice.** The custom and the law of chivalry was to give the challenge and to sound the trumpet thrice.

1223. **enforce,** difficulty.

1228. **descant,** comment from more than one point of view.

1231. **O Baal-zebub!** He is properly made to invoke Baal-zebub, as afterwards to swear by Astaroth — that is the deities of the Philistines and neighbouring nations.

1238. **bulk without spirit vast,** of vast bulk without spirit or courage.

1245. **unconscionable.** Here means "enormous' or "vast".

1248. **father of five sons.** For the story of Goliath of Gath, see *I Samuel,* xvii, and four other giants, including the brother of Goliath, are mentioned in *II Samuel,* xxii, 15-22.

1249. **Goliah.** Note Milton's spelling instead of the familiar Goliath, and *Ebrews* (l. 1308) for Hebrews.

FOURTH STASIMON — Lines 1292-1309

1309. **remark him,** mark him out, distinguish him.

FIFTH EPISODE — Lines 1310-1426

1325. **antics,** buffoons.

       mummers. A contemptuous word for "actors".

1359. **Nazarite.** See note l. 318.

1360. **Dagon.** See note l. 13.

1369. **the sentence holds,** the maxim holds good.

1377. **dispense with me,** exempt me from my duty.

1396. **engines,** methods, devices, implying "tortures".

1397. **hamper,** render powerless.

       as, so that. The sense is, "We shall find such engines . . . as will force you".

FIFTH STASIMON — Lines 1427-1440

1431. **the Angel of thy birth.** See *Judges,* xiii, 3-24.

1436. **in the camp of Dan.** See *Judges,* xiii, 25.

EXODUS — Lines 1441-1758

1445. **peace with you.** An Eastern greeting, "salaam".

1461-1471. There is a reference underneath the surface to those in power in England at the date of the poem, and the light in which they would stand in the eyes of the political party to which Milton belonged.

Some much averse . . . priests. Extreme Royalists and the High Church party.

more moderate. The Presbyterians, who had joined the Royalists.

1484. **not wanting him, I shall want nothing.** A play on the two meanings of "want".

1507. **as next,** as nearest *i.e.* of the same tribe.

1508. **Oh, what noise!** "It should be observed with what art and judgment Milton prepares the reader for the relation of the catastrophe of this tragedy. This abrupt start of Manoah upon hearing the hideous noise, and the description of it by the Chorus in their answer, in terms so full of dread and terror, naturally fill the mind with a presaging horror proper for the occasion.

"This is still kept up by their suspense and reasoning about it, and at last raised to a proper pitch by the frighted and distracted manner of the Messenger's coming in, and in his hesitation and backwardness in telling what had happened. What gives it the greater strength and beauty is the sudden transition from that soothing and flattering prospect with which Manoah was entertaining his thoughts, to a scene so totally opposite" (Thyer).

1512. **inhabitation,** mass of inhabitants.

1529. **dole,** woe, as from a warrior striking ("dealing") blows.

1538. **post.** speedily, post-haste. In Milton's day fresh horses were kept at "posts" at regular intervals along a road: a traveller rode more quickly on relays of fresh horses.

baits, delays (for refreshments).

1556. **distract,** distracted (by the calamity),

1574. **windy,** empty, vain, consisting of air alone.

1600. **abroad,** See note l. 919.

1607. **degree Of sort,** rank of the quality.

1610. **banks,** benches.

scaffolds, raised platforms (to give a good view).

1619. **cataphracts,** men on horses, both in complete armour.

spears, spearmen (metonymy).

1621. **Rifted,** tore or rent asunder.

1641. **reason,** reasonable.

1645. **strike.** An ironical play on the word.

1667. **in number . . . before.** See *Judges,* xvi, 30.

1669. **sublime,** uplifted.

1670. **Drunk with idolatry.** An allusion to *Isaiah,* xxix, 9.

1674. **Silo.** Shiloh, the place where the tabernacle and the ark then were. See *Joshua,* xviii, 1.

1680. **unweetingly,** unwittingly.

1688. **thought,** considered to be, regarded as.

1692. **as an evening dragon . . . heads.** The two similes in these lines are in antithesis — his coming was that of a serpent ("dragon") on the ground, but it was as an eagle that he swooped down on their heads to destroy them.

1695. **villatic,** barn-door, belonging to a farm-house.

1696. **cloudless.** And therefore unexpected. One would not expect thunder when the sky is clear.

1697. **given for,** considered as. *Cf.* 1. 121.

1697-1707. The construction is — thus Virtue (personified), when given up for lost, like the Phœnix, reviving out of her very ashes, flourishes again, and though her body die, her fame lives for ages. The Phœnix was a fabulous Arabian bird, only one of which ever existed, and as each Phœnix died a new bird rose from its decomposing body ("ashy womb").

1700. **embost,** hidden, sheltered in a wood, covered with foliage.

1702. **holocaust,** *lit.* a "whole" burnt offering, a sacrifice in which the victim was burnt entire.

1703. **teemed,** born (again).

1713. **sons of Caphtor.** Philistines. Caphtor (or Caphtotim) is thrice mentioned as an early settlement of the Philistines. See *Deuteronomy,* ii, 23.

1732. **obsequy,** funeral rites, usually now only in the plural — "obsequies".

1734. **shade . . . palm.** The laurel and the palm were symbols of victory. In a hot country trees were valued for their shade.

1746. **dispose,** dispensation. *Cf.* "disposition", 1. 373.

1751. **in place,** being present, by his presence.

1753. **band them,** band (or banded) themselves together.

1755. **his servants.** Manoa and the Chorus.
acquist. An old form of "acquisition".

QUESTIONS

GENERAL QUESTIONS

1. Comment, with brief quotations, on any passages of *Samson Agonistes* which refer to Milton's own experience.

2. Indicate the extent to which Milton has introduced (a) his own views, (b) references to the life of his time.

3. Show how this poem illustrates (a) Milton's love of liberty, (b) his anger with those who interfere with it.

4. Estimate briefly the extent of Milton's reading, so far as it may be judged from *Samson Agonistes*.

5. How do Samson's interviews with (a) Manoa, (b) Dalila, (c) Harapha, forward the development of the plot?

6. Contrast the scene in which Manoa first appears with that in which he appears at the end.

7. Give the substance of (a) Sampson's lament over his blindness, (b) the messenger's description of the scene in the Temple, quoting from each a passage which seems to you specially notable as poetry and giving reasons for your choice.

8. Which do you think are the three greatest speeches or passages of dialogue in *Samson Agonistes?* Justify your choice with the help of illustrative quotation, and give a detailed account of one of them.

9. What qualities of *Samson Agonistes* show Milton to be (a) a picturesque poet, (b) a musical poet?

10. Discuss Milton's similes.

11. The chief merits of *Samson Agonistes* are considered to be (a) the poignant personal element, (b) loftiness of tone, (c) imaginative splendour, (d) majesty of sound, (e) moral earnestness. Give an example of each. Can you add to the list?

12. The poem is usually censured on the grounds that (a) it is lacking in dramatic qualities, (b) it has great diffuseness, (c) the plot is inclined to "drag", (d) signs of the increasing age of the poet, with a loss of critical acumen are apparent.

13. Harmony is found in *Samson Agonistes* — harmony between passionate feelings and utterances, between the sense of a passage and its rhythm. Give three or four illustrations to prove that this is a true statement.

14. In tragedies we often find examples of "tragic irony" (*i.e.* when a character in a play speaks words which have one meaning for him and a further meaning for the spectators, who know what has happened or is about to happen). What examples of "tragic irony" can you find in *Samson Agonistes?*

15. Illustrate and comment on Milton's use of (a) blank verse, (b) lyric passages in the play.

16. The last lines of *Samson Agonistes* (1708-1758) were set as a test piece in a verse-speaking contest at Oxford some years ago. Explain fully why you think that this piece was chosen.

17. Tennyson called Milton a "mighty-mouthed inventor of harmonies". Show by comment on *your* quotations from *Samson Agonistes* (from different parts of the poem) how you interpret this.

18. Which two episodes in the play would you read to a friend in order to encourage him (her) to study the whole? Account for your choice.

19. Show the influence of Milton's classical scholarship in his imagery, diction and sentence-structure.

20. Though the *form* of the play is influenced by Greek literature, the *feeling* is Hebrew. Show that this is true by referring to the structure of *Samson Agonistes* and to the conversations that take place.

21. Point out the main features of the dramatic structure of *Samson Agonistes*.

22. Examine the function of the Chorus in *Samson Agonistes*.

23. Discuss the character of Samson as it appears to Samson himself.

24. Describe the character of Samson as seen through the eyes of (a) Dalila, (b) Harapha.

25. What evidence of deep religious feeling do you find in (a) Samson, (b) Manoa?

26. Which of the characters other than Samson do you find the most attractive? Give reasons for your answer.

27. Show how Dalila reveals her character in her interview with Samson.

28. Illustrate from the play the qualities of (a) courage, and (b) sympathy.

29. How far is it reasonable to approach *Samson Agonistes* as a stage-play and to criticise it accordingly?

30. It is sometimes said that Milton has no attraction for the present age. Do you think that there are any reasons for considering this a false statement, especially in regard to *Samson Agonistes*?

CONTEXT QUESTIONS

1. But who is this, what thing of sea or land?
    Female of sex it seems,
    That, so bedecked, ornate, and gay,
    Comes this way, sailing
    Like a stately ship
    Of Tarsus, bound for the isles
    Of Javan or Gadire,
    With all her bravery on, and tackle trim,
    Sails filled, and streamers waving
    Courted by all the winds that hold them play; . . .

    (a) Complete the description of Dalila.

    (b) Where are Tarsus, the isles of Javan, Gadire?

    (c) What do you understand by "bravery"?

    (d) Summarise the effect upon Samson of the visit of Dalila.

    (e) In what way is this simile typical of Milton? Mention another simile of the same kind in the poem.

    (f) What qualities of Milton's imagination are shown in this description?

2. To please thy gods thou didst it; gods unable
    To acquit themselves and prosecute their foes
    But by ungodly deeds, *the contradiction*
    Of their own deity, gods cannot be;
    Less therefore to be pleased, obeyed, or feared.
    These false pretexts and varnished colours failing,
    Bare in thy guilt, how foul must thou appear!

    (a) "Thou didst it." Didst what?

    (b) "These false pretexts." What false pretexts?

    (c) What do you understand by "varnished colours"?

    (d) Explain in your own words the meaning of the passage in italics.

    (e) What has led to this outburst, and what is the outcome of the dialogue in which it occurs?

3. O miserable change! is this the man,

    . . . .
    . . . . who, single combatant,
    Duelled their armies ranked in proud array,
    Himself an army, now unequal match
    To save himself against a coward armed
    At one spear's length?

    (a) By whom are these words spoken and upon what occasion?

    (b) What particular exploits of Samson previous to his blindness are mentioned in different parts of the play?

    (c) Would you say that the metaphor in this passage was typical of Milton?

4. But he, though blind of sight,
Despised, and thought extinguished quite,
With inward eyes illuminated,
His fiery virtue roused
From under ashes into sudden flame,
And as an evening dragon came,
Assailant on the perched roosts
And nests in order ranged
Of tame villatic fowl; but as an eagle
His cloudless thunder bolted on their heads.

    (a) Point out an example of (i) antithesis, (ii) a metaphor, (iii) a simile, (iv) a metaphor within a simile.

    (b) Do you think that the two similes are appropriate?

    (c) Comment briefly on the range of the subject-matter of Milton's similes in the poem.

    (d) Why *"cloudless* thunder"?

    (e) The metre of this passage is different from that of the bulk of the poem. Say what you consider the reason for the difference, and explain wherein it consists.

5. His ransom, if my whole inheritance
May compass it, shall willingly be paid
And numbered down; much rather I shall choose
To live the poorest in my tribe, than richest,
And he in that calamitous prison left.
No, I am fixed not to part hence without him.
For his redemption all my patrimony.
If need be, I am ready to forgo
And quit; not wanting him, I shall want nothing.

    (a) What else does Manoa offer to do for Samson?

    (b) What comment does the Chorus make on Manoa's offer in the passage above?

    (c) What light do these words throw on his character?

    (d) Comment on the phraseology of the last line.

6. Had not his prowess quelled their pride
    In that sore battle, when so many died
    Without reprieve, adjudged to death,
    For want of well pronouncing *Shibboleth*.

    (a) "His prowess." Whose prowess?
    (b) In what way did he defend Israel other than by force of
        arms?
    (c) Tell the well-known Bible story to which the last line refers.
    (d) The word "Shibboleth" has become proverbial in the Eng-
        lish language. Explain its application.

7. I was to do my part from Heaven assigned,
    And had performed it, if my known offence
    Had not disabled me, not all your force.
    These shifts refuted, answer thy appellant,
    Though by his blindness maimed for high attempts,
    Who now defies thee thrice to single fight,
    As a petty enterprise of small enforce.

    (a) What was the "known offence"?
    (b) What do you understand by "of small enforce"?
    (c) Why was the challenge said to be given "thrice"?
    (d) What was the answer to this challenge?

8.   Little I had despatched,
    When all abroad was rumoured that this day
    Samson should be brought forth to show the people
    Proof of his mighty strength in feats and games.
    I sorrowed at his captive state, but minded
    Not to be absent at that spectacle.
    The building was a spacious theatre.

    (a) Was the rumour correct?
    (b) Explain the meaning of "abroad".
    (c) Describe the theatre, saying how the accommodation for the
        lords differed from that for the common people.

9. Yet, knowing their advantages too many,
    Because they shall not trail me through their streets
    Like a wild beast, I am content to go.
    Masters' commands come with a power resistless
    To such as owe them absolute subjection;
    And for a life who will not change his purpose?
    (So mutable are all the ways of men!)

Yet this be sure, in nothing to comply
Scandalous or forbidden in our law.

(a) "To go." Go where?

(b) Express the two lines in italics in your own words.

(c) "Our law." What sense do these words bear?

(d) Give another instance of Samson's obedience to the "law".

(e) One line is a mere pretext, to allay suspicion. Which line? How is it proved to be a pretext later in the play?

(f) What is the connection of the sentence in brackets with the rest of the argument?

10. See how he lies at random, carelessly diffused,
With languished head unpropped,
As one past hope, abandoned,
And by himself given over;
In slavish habit, ill-fitted weeds,
O'er-worn and soiled.

(a) Describe Samson's appearance in your own words.

(b) Mention one or two of Samson's former exploits which are given as a contrast with his present helplessness.

(c) Comment upon the irregular metre of these lines.

(d) In not more than two sentences summarise the subject-matter of the Chorus in which this passage occurs.

11.   But cords to me were threads
Touched with the flame; on their whole host I flew
Unarmed, and with a trivial weapon felled
Their choicest youth; they only lived who fled.
Had Judah that day joined, or one whole tribe,
They had by this possessed the towers of Gath,
And lorded over them whom now they serve.

(a) What was the "trivial weapon"? Tell the story briefly.

(b) Where was Gath? Mention any character in the play who came from there.

(c) Why does the form or shortness of the metaphor in this passage make it more vivid in its context? Have you any other comment to pass on this metaphor?

12. His servants He, with new acquist
Of true experience from this great event,
With peace and consolation hath dismissed,
And calm of mind, all passion spent.

(a) "His servants." Which in particular?

(b) What do you understand by "acquist"?

(c) What is the effect of the quiet and confident ending of *Samson Agonistes*?

(d) Comment on its literary and dramatic value.

(e) Can you give an example from the work of any other poet of a quiet ending after strain and stress?

13.   O glorious strength,
Put to the labour of a beast, debased
Lower than bondslave! Promise was that I
Should Israel from Philistian yoke deliver;
Ask for this great deliverer now, and find him
Eyeless in Gaza, at the mill with slaves,
Himself in bonds under Philistian yoke.
Yet stay, let me not rashly call in doubt
Divine prediction.

(a) Why did Samson think it rash to "call in doubt divine prediction"?

(b) Which of his afflictions does Samson count the greatest? Quote one or two lines supporting your answer, if you can.

(c) Point out the alliteration in this passage.

14. Comes he in peace? What wind hath blown him hither
I less conjecture than when first I saw
The sumptuous Dalila floating this way;
His habit carries peace, his brow defiance.

   Samson. Or peace or not, alike to me he comes.

   Chorus. His fraught we soon shall know; he now arrives.

(a) "Comes he in peace?" Answer this question.

(b) How was he recognized at a distance?

(c) Put Samson's comment into your own words.

(d) What is the meaning of "fraught"?

(e) In what way is the beginning of this Episode similar to that of most of the others?

(f) What was the effect upon Samson of this visit?

15. Wilt thou then serve the Philistines with that gift
Which was expressly given thee to annoy them?
Better at home lie bed-rid, not only idle,

Inglorious, unemployed, with age outworn.
But God, who caused a fountain at thy prayer
From the dry ground to spring, thy thirst to allay
After the brunt of battle, can as easy
Cause light again within thy eyes to spring,
Wherewith to serve Him better than thou hast;
And I persuade me so; why else . . .

(a) "That gift." Which gift?
(b) What is the meaning of "annoy"?
(c) "But God . . . battle." When was this?
(d) "Why else. . . ." How does he illustrate his argument?

KEY TO CONTEXT QUESTIONS
(1) ll. 710-719; (2) 896-902; (3) 340, 344-348; (4) 1687-1696; (5) 1476-1484; (6) 286-289; (7) 1217-1223; (8) 1599-1605, (9) 1401-1409; (10) 118-123, (11) 261-267; (12) 1755-1758; (13) 36-44; (14) 1070-1075; (15) 577-586.

SONG ON MAY MORNING
A fine lyric in the Jonsonian manner without the tortured conceits of the metaphysical school. Like the later *L'Allegro* and *Il Penseroso*, Milton uses eight-syllable lines.

THE PASSION
The poem is unfinished, and also unworthy of its author. He cannot seem to inspire any feeling for the theme of Christ's resurrection after death. He suggests that the salvation of man depends not only on Christ but on man himself.

TO THE NIGHTINGALE
Milton evidently had an affection for the nightingale; he refers to it in *Il Penseroso* and in *Comus*. This is evidently an early sonnet written by the "lady of Christ's" not the severe-looking man that Milton later became. It was probably composed either at Cambridge or at Horton and illustrates quite clearly Milton's youthfulness and his love of Nature. An old legend declares that the lover who hears the nightingale before the cuckoo will have his love returned. The nightingale is there, therefore, connected with joy, though later poets such as Keats and Matthew Arnold have shown its affinity with sad happenings.

The sonnet is of the Petrarchan type, the rhyme-scheme being *abba, abba, cd, cd, cd*. There is no apparent break between the octave and the sextet.

Milton begins with an apostrophe to the bird and stresses the personal note by asking it to sing earlier than the cuckoo does during this particular year in order to convince him of success in love.

yon: The use of this word signifies distance.

bloomy: covered with blossom.

spray: branch.

the words are still: the other birds have gone to rest.

jolly hours: "jolly" is connected with the French "joli" = "pretty," and here means "festive"; its modern meaning suggests more robustious mirth. The Hours or Horæ were goddesses connected with the different seasons.

that close the eye of day: The suggestion is here made that the pleasing notes of the nightingale send the day to sleep.

propitious May: May was supposed to be a favourable month for lovers.

shallow cuckoo's bill: The song of the cuckoo which is unmusical and only merits contempt for its lack of fullness. "Bill" is really the beak of the bird but is used here to represent the sound that comes out of the beak.

portend: foretell.

Jove: the chief of the gods.

amorous power: power over the affairs of those in love.

timely: at the proper time, i.e. before the cuckoo begins.

bird of hate: bird which is hated. The cuckoo is disliked by the other birds.

as: because.

yet hadst no reason why: it is difficult to account for the fact that in the last few years you seem to have come after the cuckoo.

the Muse: the Muse of Poetry.

his mate: The use of the masculine possessive pronoun shows that the nightingale is considered as feminine. It is curious though that in this way a Muse is considered to be masculine.

train: following. Milton shows in the line in which this word occurs that he is interested in love and devoted to poetry.

TO A VIRTUOUS YOUNG LADY

It is not known whether Milton had any particular lady in mind when he wrote this sonnet. An idea is sometimes put forward that it was addressed to a certain Miss Davis, a lady in whose company Milton took pleasure, and colour is lent to this suggestion by the date of the sonnet which is generally fixed at 1644, a time when Milton's wife refused to return to him.

The rhyme-scheme is *abba, abba, cde, cde*. The rhyming of the 1st, 4th, 5th and 8th lines is not really good for there is a decided difference in pronunciation between "youth," "Truth," " Ruth" and "ruth." The metaphor taken from the Bible of the Bridegroom and the Wise Virgin is notable, and other Biblical allusions occur in the names Mary and Ruth.

the prime: the best time.

the broad way and the green: a reference to the Bible story of those who take the "broad way" that leads to destruction and the "narrow" way that leads to eternal life. St. Matthew vii. 13.

the better part: Christ said that Mary in choosing to listen to his words had chosen a "better part" than her sister Martha, who was encumbered by household cares. S. Luke, x, 42.

Ruth: Ruth, the gleaner, was devoted to her mother-in-law, Naomi, and refused to be parted from her even though her constancy entailed her travelling to a distant country. The story is told in the Book of Ruth.

overween: become too proud.

spleen: anger. The spleen is a part of the body which sometimes suffers disturbance when emotion is aroused.

odorous lamp: the lamp, filled with oil, that was carried by each of the wise Virgins who prepared themselves to meet the Bridegroom. The parable is told in St. Matthew, xxv, 1-13.

TO THE LADY MARGARET LEY

Milton seemed to have a real affection for the children of his friends and here he declares that the virtues of the Earl of Marlborough live on in his daughter Margaret. James Ley, who was afterwards created Earl of Marlborough by Charles I, was Lord High Treasurer of England and Lord President of the Council. He was an incorruptible statesman and it was he who passed the sentence on Bacon for bribery. His daughter married Captain Hobson; they lived near Milton in Aldersgate Street, London, and both were very fond of the Puritan poet. The sonnet was written probably in 1644 or 1645.

Sad breaking of that Parliament broke him: a play upon words. After the Petition of Rights, 1628, there was a breach between Charles and those Parliamentary leaders such as Marlborough who upheld the Petition.

Chaeronea: in Northern Greece. Alexander the Great subjugated Greece in 338 B.C.

Old man eloquent: Isocrates, the Athenian orator, who at the age of 98 committed suicide, according to tradition on hearing of the defeat at Chaeronea.

TO MR. H. LAWES ON HIS AIRS

Henry Lawes (1595-1662) who composed the music for *Comus* and *Arcades,* and who acted in both these masques is said to have been one of the first English musicians to study the proper accentuation of words. The sonnet was written in 1645, but first appeared as a prefix to *Choice Psalms, put into music for Three Voices, composed by Henry and William Lawes, Brothers and Servants to his Majesty,* 1648. Though Lawes was a Royalist his friendship with Milton was unbroken, and one of their great ties was a common love of music. In this sonnet Milton stresses his friend's skill in adapting his music to the rhythm of the words he uses.

The form of the sonnet is Petrarchan, the rhyme-scheme being *abba, abba, cde, dce.*

Midas ears: asses ears, denoting want of intelligence. Midas, the king of Phrygia, was once appointed judge in a musical contest between Apollo and Pan. He gave the prize to Pan, whereupon Apollo, in indignation, changed his ears into those of an ass.

committing short and long: bringing together short and long syllables, i.e. according to the English method of scansion accented and unaccented syllables.

wan: pale.

could humour bestow tongue: could make your music suit the English language.

the priest of Phoebus' quire: the leader of the choir of Apollo, i.e. Phæbus.

hymn or story: Lawes set to music the story of "Ariadne," written by a friend named Cartwright.

Dante: an Italian poet who wrote the "Divine Comedy" composed of the "Purgatorio," the "Inferno" and the "Paradiso."

Casella: a Florentine musician.

wooed to sing: Dante is supposed to have met Casella in Purgatory and to have begged him to sing. Casella responded by singing one of Dante's own songs.

milder shades of Purgatory: Dante is supposed to have come from the inferno, a very dreadful place, therefore he found Purgatory considerably pleasanter than his previous abode.

TO THE LORD GENERAL FAIRFAX

This sonnet, like certain other sonnets referring to political personages was not published during the lifetime of Milton. Most of his minor poems came out in a second edition in 1673, but these did not appear until in 1694 a memoir of Milton was published. It would not have been safe to issue to Restoration readers such unqualified praise of their previous opponents. Milton, in this sonnet, pays a tribute to the success of Fairfax on a particular occasion, *viz.* when he besieged Colchester in 1648, and expresses the hope that his high character which has served him so well in his generalship will also be shown in his political life. The Petrarchan sonnet has as its rhyme-scheme: *abba, abba, cdd, cdc.*

name in arms: reputation as a soldier.

her jealous monarchs: the kings of Europe.

amaze: consternation.

new rebellions: during the siege of Colchester which Fairfax was carrying out so well there were various risings in Wales, Essex, Kent and the West of England. These risings really constituted the Second Civil War.

Their hydra heads: The Hydra was a monster with nine heads. As one was struck off two grew in its place. Hercules destroyed the monster by burning each stump which was left when he had cut off a head.

the false North displays her broken league: The Scots were waging war against the Parliamentarians while Fairfax was besieging Colchester. They are considered by Milton to have broken their part of the bargain made in the Solemn League and Covenant.

to imp their serpent wings: to strengthen the English Royalists. The Hydra was a sort of dragon or winged serpent. To "imp" is to strengthen. It refers to a graft or shoot, so the reference is to a hawk's broken wing which can be imped or strengthened by new feathers being grafted on to it.

public faith cleared from the shameful brand of public fraud: the Army leaders charged Parliament with misappropriating War Funds and taking bribes from Royalists.

TO THE LORD GENERAL CROMWELL, MAY 16, 1652
On the Proposals of Certain Ministers of the Committee for the Propagation of the Gospel

This sonnet was written before Milton had come into close connection with Cromwell. It is not only an excellent tribute to a great man who, a year later, was to become Protector of the Realm of England, but a special appeal on behalf of matters connected with the Church. Just at this time affairs of the Church were in a state of chaos. Some people wanted a State Church because many of the parishes were without clergymen, others were under Independent or Presbyterian ministers and still others had kept the parish priests who had held the livings in the time of Charles I. Milton, however, was greatly opposed to the establishment of a State Church and in this sonnet he asks Cromwell to preserve religious liberty, expressing the hope that the Lord General will be as victorious in settling the problems of peace as he was in waging the war. The rhyme-scheme is of an unusual form in the sextet, it is *abba, abba, cdd, cee.*

on the neck of crowned Fortune proud: a reference to the death of Charles I. It is on the analogy of the words in Genesis xlix, 8, "Thy hand shall be on the neck of thine enemies."

God's trophies: the works that show the greatness of God.

his work pursued: has pursued his work.

Darwen stream: The Darwen is a small river which enters the River Ribble near Preston. In 1648 Cromwell fought a three days' battle here and defeated the Scots who were invading England.

imbrued: stained.

Dunbar field: at Dunbar Cromwell defeated the Scots in 1650, but they were not finally crushed until the Battle of Worcester.

resounds: this verb, though singular in form, is really connected with the three nouns "stream," "field" and "wreath."

Worcester's laureate wreath: the Battle of Worcester was fought on September 3, 1651. This was the crowning victory for Cromwell because after it the cause of the Royalists was utterly ruined. The "laureate" wreath is one composed of laurels, the sign of victory. Our title "Poet Laureate" is taken from the custom of presenting a laurel wreath to a victor.

secular chains: the bonds of a State Church.

Help us: here we see Milton's definite appeal to Cromwell for the absolute separation of Church and State.

hireling wolves: Milton had great contempt for all those who just joined the Church in order to get money for their services. The reference is to St. John x, 12. "He that is an hireling . . . seeth the wolf coming and leaveth the sheep and fleeth." Milton's idea was that those who wanted to get the money of the Church into their own hands were like hirelings in their greed and like wolves in their persecution of other people. In "Lycidas" he pointed out that many of the Anglican clergymen "creep and intrude and climb into the fold."

maw: stomach. The meaning here is "desire" or "appetite."

TO SIR HENRY VANE THE YOUNGER

This sonnet is also concerned with the discussion about Church and State about which Milton felt so keenly. Here he asks Vane, then in his fortieth year, to be a champion of freedom of conscience in religious matters. Sir Henry Vane was born in 1612 and was beheaded in 1662 on account of his republican sympathies. He was called "the Younger" because his father was still alive. When quite young he had a successful career as Governor of Massachusetts in America, and at the age of 27 he became M.P. for Hull. When this sonnet was written he was a member of the Council of State. The sonnet follows the usual Petrarchan form, the rhyme-scheme being *abba, abba, cde, cde.*

the helm of Rome: a metaphor taken from the guiding of a ship.

gowns not arms: the wisdom of senators not the strategy of generals. This administrative ability on the part of the Roman Senators really caused the peace which followed a war of invasion to be entirely in favour of Rome, the invaded province.

The fierce Epirot: Pyrrhus, King of Epirus (318-272 B.C.) a great general who invaded Rome in 280 B.C.

The African bold: Hannibal of Carthage (247-183 B.C.) who fought against Rome from B.C. 219 until his death.

the drift of hollow states: the meaning of insincere politicians.

hard to be spelled: not easily understood.

iron and gold: arms and money, both necessary for war.

equipage: necessary materials.

bounds of either sword: the limits of the power of the Church and of the State.

TO MR. LAWRENCE

One of Milton's best friends was Edward Lawrence, son of the Lord President of the Council during the time of the Commonwealth. The poet looks forward to a meeting with Lawrence, when the two may "waste a sullen day," feasting lightly and enjoying pleasant pastimes. He advises his friend to relax from the cares of the day. Milton, of course, is not suggesting mere idleness of no account. It is a relaxation today considered cultured and refined. "Wine and song" are not to be interpreted as libidinous and Bacchanalian. The wise men, he thinks, can judge just what are limits of leisure and relaxation, and he can also partake of them often amid the toils of daily living. Note that the severe Milton is somewhat "easier" here, exuding a pleasant gentleness and understanding not usually associated with the humorless Puritan.

TO CYRIACK SKINNER

Like the previous one, this sonnet shows Milton in a mood of cheerful friendliness and also indicates his familiarity with the works of Horace. Cyriack Skinner was the grandson of Sir Edward Coke, the famous judge, who lived in the reign of Elizabeth, James I, and Charles I, and was responsible for many legal works. Milton here suggests that his friend should put aside his study of politics, mathematics, and science and enjoy the hours of leisure that are sent by God.

Themis: the Greek goddess of Law.

Euclid: a Greek geometrician.

Archimedes: a Greek physicist.

What the Swede intends and what the French: at that time the Swedes were fighting with the Poles and the French were carrying on war in the Spanish Netherlands.

TO THE SAME (CYRIACK SKINNER)

This second sonnet to Cyriack Skinner was written three years after Milton had become blind, *i.e.* in 1655. It expresses the same fortitude as is shown in Milton's sonnet *On his Blindness*. It, like the sonnets on Fairfax, Cromwell and Vane, could not be published during Milton's lifetime because it contains too definite an allusion to his political creed. In it he says that he is supported by the fact that he lost his sight in the defence of liberty and is certain that this will be a consolation to him throughout his life. The rhyme-scheme is that used in many of the sonnets, *abba, abba, cdc, dcd*. As in the sonnet *On his Blindness,* the thought changes in the middle from grief at his great handicap to life to the feeling that he has lost his sight in a good cause — in upholding the rights of man and defending liberty of the people.

though clear to outward view: though apparently uninjured. It was not easy to detect from a casual glance that Milton was blind.

bereft: deprived.

idle orbs: useless eyeballs.

bate a jot of heart or hope: diminish in the least my faith or my hope.

conscience: knowledge.

overplied: overworked.

Liberty's defence, my noble task: a reference to Milton's pamphlet "Defensio pro Populo Anglicano" published in 1651. This was written in answer to a pamphlet by Salmasius condemning the execution of Charles I. When Milton started to write this pamphlet he had lost the use of his left eye and his doctors warned him that if he persisted in finishing it he would become totally blind. However, he insisted in carrying out this work as he felt it was for the benefit of the English people.

mask: pageant or masquerade.

UPON THE CIRCUMCISION

Like the *Passion,* this effort in the religious sphere lacks reality and real emotion. It is an attempt at the grand style later used so brilliantly in the epic poems.

WHEN THE ASSAULT WAS INTENDED TO THE CITY

This sonnet was written when Milton was living at Aldersgate Street, London. The Royalist forces had marched as far as Hounslow and Brentford and were threatening the city, which was barricaded against attack in November, 1642, after the Battle of Edgehill. Milton had been active in writing pamphlets on the side of Parliament, so he may have felt that his house was really in danger of attack, though the poem seems to be written in a half-jesting spirit. In pleading with the Royalist commander — whether he be Captain or Colonel or Knight — to spare his home he quotes precedents to show that poets were held in respect by military authorities in ancient times. The assault was never carried out, as the Royalist army retreated when the Parliamentarians under the Earl of Essex set out to defend London.

Colonel: must be pronounced as three syllables.

Emathian Conqueror: Alexander, who in the sack of Thebes, 335 B.C., spared the house and family of Pindar. Pindar himself was not alive at the time.

Muses' bower: so Milton describes the house from which had issued some of the fiercest controversial pamphlets.

Pindarus: a Greek lyric writer, chiefly renowned for his odes.

Electra's poet: Euripides, who wrote a play called Electra. When the Spartans took Athens in 404 B.C. they proposed to raze the city to the ground, but desisted when they heard the Athenians singing a chorus from Euripides' Electra.

REVIEW QUESTIONS

1. Macaulay says of *L'Allegro* and *Il Penseroso* — "These poems differ from others, as attar of roses differ from ordinary rose-water, the close packed essence from the thin diluted mixture." What does he mean by this? Do you think it is true?

2. Give illustrations to prove that Milton was a "learned" poet.

3. Collect ten of Milton's descriptive adjectives and show how appropriately they are used.

4. Tennyson calls Milton "God-gifted organ-voice of England." Use as many poems as possible to illustrate the truth of this remark.

5. What allusions are made in *Lycidas* to contemporary events and institutions?

6. What is meant by a "pastoral elegy"? How does *Lycidas* fit the description you have given of this type of poem?

7. Write appreciations of any two sonnets of Milton.

8. Show carefully how the beginnings of *L'Allegro* and *Il Penseroso* prepare us for the thought in the remainder of each poem.

9. Illustrate the mingling of Christian and pagan elements in the *Hymn on the Morning of Christ's Nativity*.

10. What do you consider are the notable features of (a) *At a Solemn Music,* (b) *Sonnet to Cyriack Skinner?*

11. Show that to some extent Milton reveals his character in the sonnets.

12. Show by reference to *L'Allegro* and *Il Penseroso* that Milton appreciated the pleasures of Nature and of Art.

13. Illustrate from as many poems as possible (a) the conciseness, (b) the splendour of Milton's style.

14. What knowledge of Milton's own character do you gain from (a) the *Nativity Ode* (b) *Lycidas*?

15. To what persons and events does Milton refer in his sonnets?

16. Consider *L'Allegro* and *Il Penseroso* as being "complementary rather than "contrasting" poems.

17. Write an essay on the poetry of Milton, arranging your material under the following headings: (a) observation of nature, (b) pictorial power, (c) philosophy.

18. What evidence is given by *L'Allegro* and *Il Penseroso* that they were written in Milton's youth?

19. What light is thrown on the history of the time by Milton's political sonnets?

20. Consider carefully the *form* of Milton's sonnets. How does he vary the rhyme-scheme in the sestet?

21. What is meant by a "tailed" sonnet? Has it any advantage over the ordinary sonnet-form?

22. How far do you think the sonnets are autobiographical?

23. What light do the sonnets throw upon (a) Milton's own views on his blindness, (b) Milton's friends, (c) Milton's theory of Church Government?

24. Illustrate from as many works of Milton as possible his love and appreciation of music.

OUTLINES OF MILTON'S MAJOR PROSE WORKS

OF REFORMATION TOUCHING CHURCH DISCIPLINE IN ENGLAND

This is probably his first real controversial piece. It is a carefully documented historical discussion of the progress of the English church from Henry VIII, and it tries to prove that the progress of the church has been hampered by groups belonging to the old Catholic sections of the church. Under Henry, Edward, and Elizabeth the Anglican Church was a result of a compromise with Catholicism, rather than of a truly Protestant reformation. He argues here against the principle of episcopacy; instead, he prefers a government made up of "synods." Real truth and simplicity are found in the Gospel and not in the distortions of theological controversy. He also inveighs against the corruption of the clergy. In the final section, he becomes eloquent in a passage of reverent prayer asking for the deliverance of England from ecclesiastical tyranny. Milton, in this anti-prelatical tract, favors the Presbyterian form of church government. He would abolish bishops, and would model the church after Scotch Presbyterianism.

OF PRELATICAL EPISCOPACY

This is a defence of Milton's position. It is a pamphlet refuting point by point the authorities listed by Archbishop Ussher to prove that the institution of bishops was an institution of the primitive church. Episcopacy cannot be deduced from ancient history of the church. Milton's knowledge of church history is immense.

THE REASON OF CHURCH GOVERNMENT URGED AGAINST PRELATY

Again Milton argues for the Presbyterian as against the Episcopal system. In this treatise, the longest and perhaps the best of all his ecclesiastical tracts he argues systematically that the gospel prescribes the Presbyterian system; that Prelacy is against the very spirit of Christianity, with its love of elaborate display, rites, and symbolisms. Here he also enunciates one of his cardinal beliefs, namely, the separation of Church and State. Neither does he believe in the existence of only one sect. Uniformity of belief is not to be enforced; the variety of sects is a good omen that real reform is taking place, and here he hints at one of the main themes of his *Areopagitica.* The individual is to determine the form of his belief; no intermediaries are essential or desirable, and man's conscience alone must be the deciding judge as to the nature of his spiritual state. A digression occurs in the beginning of Book II that is interesting for its autobiographical element; he says that he intends to write an epic poem after he has done his duty in purifying religion. The whole tenor of the argument of this treatise leads to an advocacy of free speech and liberty, a liberty that is disciplined, however. True liberty consists in order — an order based on logic and reason.

AN APOLOGY AGAINST A PAMPHLET A MODEST CONFUTATION OF THE ANIMADVERSIONS OF THE REMONSTRANT AGAINST SMECTYMNUUS

In this tract, Milton denunciates the attack made on his private life by Bishop Hall and his son. The violence of his abuse is compensated for by the self-vindication in which Milton gives us information of his early life, studies, and temperament. This pamphlet is most personal, and, despite the lapse of reason in the virulence of the invective directed against his enemies, it holds an important niche in the body of his prose work.

THE DOCTRINE AND DISCIPLINE OF DIVORCE

This and the next few tracts deal with the divorce laws, and they were occasioned, undoubtedly, by Milton's own difficulties in his married life with Mary Powell. Desiring to marry again, he felt the need of justifying his action and of obtaining more liberal divorce laws. The salient theme is that the differences of minds, the "contrariety of minds," or incompatibility, as we call it today, is a fair and just basis for divorce. No real marriage can exist without it; a marriage should be dissolved upon proof of incompatibility. Marriage is spiritual as well as physical and it is wrong to think that it is dissoluble only on physical grounds alone. He was disgusted with the idea that two people could be externally forced to live together when mutual bonds of love and understanding were absent. He tried to show that the Scriptures agreed with him in this matter. The substance of marriage, he maintained, is superior to its form. Marriage being a private affair, it could be, and should be, annulled by mutual consent, or even by the consent of one.

THE JUDGMENT OF MARTIN BUCER, CONCERNING DIVORCE

This tract merely uses all the relevant parts of Bucer's argument in favor of divorce. Bucer was a German Protestant clergyman who argued that incompatibility was grounds for divorce, that absolute divorce, not merely the end of living together economically and physically, should exist.

TETRACHORDEN

Again, Milton argues in like vein for divorce, but here he continues, in greater detail, the examination of Scripture dealing with the subject. (Tetrachorden is a word based on the tetrachord in music; that is, four notes represented by the string of the lyre. Milton's tract concerns the four passages in the Bible, *Genesis, Deuteronomy, The Gospel of St. Matthew,* and in the *First Epistle to the Corinthians,* that treat of the subject of divorce). All these tracts on divorce failed to reform society and its laws at that time, although in modern times we have drawn very near, or even farther from, the ideas on divorce as advocated by Milton.

OF EDUCATION

Samuel Hartlib, a fine citizen interested in educational theories and practices, requested the views of John Milton on the subject. The result was a short tractate on education, addressed to Hartlib, published anonymously in 1644. Milton had been a teacher himself, let alone a scholar. His program is an enormously difficult and broad one, and it represents, in most essentials, the type of education advocated by humanists of his period. Much of what he commends is quite modern and realistic.

Milton combines practical and ideal methods in his educational views. Textbook learning, although necessary, should be supplemented by actual contact with living, practical people, and by the contemplation of actual institutions. Empty scholastic exercises he condemns heartily. The whole aim of his educational policy is the creation of an all-round gentleman, a scholar who must be suited also for participation in public affairs, a man of the world as well as a student in the study. Such an ideal was a Renaissance conception, it is true, but Milton gives it vigor and emphasis. The complete education "fits a man to perform justly, skillfully, and magnanimously all the offices, both public and private, of peace and war." This is a large order, and Milton's prescribed course of study is strenuous indeed.

The educated man must have a good knowledge of the ancient civilization, particularly the Greek and Latin. He must apply his experience from the past to the present, making it functional thereby; the classics must be made to live. Subject matter rather than expression is to be stressed in the study of Greek and Latin. Besides, one must study Italian, Hebrew, and Syriac, as well as military discipline. The school he envisions will give a complete training to boys from twelve to twenty-one. Later, they should travel and learn from experience. Milton does not include training at a university. The subjects to be studied, the discipline and the scope of the whole plan, makes this course most difficult to carry out in practice. It is an ideal view, not easily applicable, certainly not in full, to our way of life today. It is an aristocratic program envisioning the education of the higher classes trained to become leaders in the public affairs of the day. But it does brand Milton as an intense believer in the powers of education.

Milton advises that one should begin by learning good grammar; inculcate a love of learning in yourself. Arithmetic and geometry should be taught, and the Scriptures studied in the evening. Now comes the study of agriculture, with Cato, Varro, Calumella as authorities, and the reading of the Greek authors, as Aristotle's *Historical Physiology* in the original. Engineering, philosophy, and architecture, together with medicine, should be learned. Virgil, Orpheus, and other classicists should be read. Plato, Xenophon, Cicero, and Plutarch should be studied for the art of reasoning. Then comes the study of economics, together with law. Theology should be taken up in the evenings. Next come Attic tragedies, heroic poems, political orations, etc. It is necessary to cultivate the Art of Poetry, and the Art of Composition.

Diet and exercise must be given some attention, fencing, wrestling, and other sports. Music, too, must be given some attention; communion with nature and bubbling with goodness, must be obtained by excursions into the fields.

AREOPAGITICA

THE SUBJECT

No more powerful defence of the liberty of the press has been written in this country than Milton's *Areopagitica*.

Perhaps we are apt to take freedom of expression for granted, and it comes as a shock to learn from a report in 1956 that only four countries in the world have the advantage of it in the press. We know that Fascist and Nazi tyrannies dared not tolerate it, that Communism has not yet tolerated freedom of expression in speech, print, or any form of art, and that the policy of certain religious orders, predominantly the Catholic, is to canalize thought by banning books and other publications expressing views contrary to established beliefs. Exacerbated racial prejudices have aggravated intolerance in certain countries, and it is no exaggeration to say that the question of liberty of thought and expression is one of the most momentous issues in the world to-day. As such it was given pride of place among the four freedoms which President Roosevelt promulgated in 1941 as the only basis for the security of all peoples.

Alien as this freedom is to the vast majority of the people of the world to-day, it has been regarded for centuries as an integral feature and requisite of English democracy. For freedom in the widest and most rational sense of the word English people have struggled for centuries; in defence of it they have fought at home and abroad; and millions have crossed the Atlantic from Great Britain and Europe to establish or join a new order where all shall be free. The first of them left this country not many years before Milton wrote his challenging demand for the freedom of the press in 1644.

Milton did not proclaim a belief in absolute freedom. He wanted only "rational liberty" (*Paradise Lost,* XII, 82). He did not believe that propaganda in favour of impiety and corruption of good manners and morals should be connived at. Nor did he believe that liberty should be extended to include complete freedom for subversive forces to destroy liberty; he would not tolerate "Popery and open superstition" for fear they should extirpate all "religious and civil supremacies". A grave problem confronting democracies of the twentieth century is to what extent forces inimical to freedom should be tolerated among freedom-loving peoples. At a time of political insecurity Milton was all for "suppressing the suppressors".

By the "press" to-day we generally mean newspapers, and it is worth noting that the struggle for the freedom of this particular medium of expression did not reach a triumphant conclusion in England until the early part of the nineteenth century, when *The Times* succeeded in freeing itself from Government controls. Wherever the liberty of the press obtains, freedom in broadcasting and television inevitably follows; contrariwise — and this applies to a greater or smaller extent in most countries — lack of freedom in the press is matched by loss of liberty in other means of appealing to the public.

In *Areopagitica* Milton appears to be concerned primarily with books and pamphlets. There is no doubt, however, that he was concerned with all forms of publication, including newspapers. For the Licensing Act of June 14, 1643, against which he was moved to protest, was directed against "false, forged, scandalous, seditious, libellous, and unlicensed Papers, Pamphlets, and Books to the defamation of Religion and government". Though news-letters in the form of "news-books" or pamphlets had been in existence, it was not until the stormy opening years of the Civil War that newspapers (weekly) as we know them took shape. Milton's plea fell on deaf ears, and it was not until 1694 that the principle that books should be published without Government control received legal sanction. Newspapers continued to struggle for independence of expression. In

1703 Defoe, who was to become famous as the author of *Robinson Crusoe,* was set in the pillory, imprisoned in Newgate, and fined for daring to launch a press attack on the Government.

Now for well over a century Governments in England have had to reckon with the voice of the people in the press; and it was because of the emergence of this new medium for political pressure on behalf of democratic rights and truth that the historian Macaulay, with the three estates of pre-Revolutionary France — the nobility, the Church, and the people — in mind, dubbed it "the fourth estate".

THE TITLE

In writing *Areopagitica,* Milton was inspired by the example of Isocrates ("that old man eloquent" of the sonnet *To the Lady Margaret Ley*), who appealed in his *Areopagiticos* for a revival of the old Athenian order of justice and democracy when Athens was threatened by Philip of Macedon: "I could name him who from his private house wrote that discourse to the Parliament of Athens, that persuades them to change the form of democracy which was then established." The judges of the Areopagus or Hill of Mars were chosen for their virtues; they were the arbiters of justice and preservers of morals and civil liberty. The only books they suppressed were "either blasphemous and atheistical, or libellous" (p. 30). As Isocrates had appealed for a revival of democracy through the re-establishment of the Court of the Areopagus, so Milton appeals to the Long Parliament to sponsor "rational liberty".

There the parallel ends for the Greek orator demands a tightening of the moral order, whereas Milton asks for relaxation of press control in the conviction that truth will prevail. Moreover, Isocrates' oration was compiled with indefatigable attention to stylistic merit throughout, whereas Milton's work shows evidence of impetuosity and carelessness; it is very uneven, at times magnificently inspired, at times unnecessarily labyrinthine, and generally giving the impression of improvisation and accumulation — sometimes disproportionate and repetitive — within a simple plan.

THE NATIONAL BACKGROUND TO AREOPAGITICA

A rigid press censorship derives from fear and, except in established democracies, is likely to arise when any Government feels insecure. As this fear recedes, press control generally relaxes.

To understand why *Areopagitica* was written in 1644 it is necessary to know the main principles at stake in the struggle between king and Parliament. It would be a mistake to think that the quarrel was directly between Charles I and the common people. The struggle lay between him and the rich commercial and landed classes; after the execution of Charles in 1649, Cromwell became so unpopular that the restoration of the monarchy brought general relief. Nevertheless, the people's passions and, in particular, their religious prejudices were exploited against Charles I. The king aimed at making England strong, but he was handicapped by, among other things, lack of financial resources. He was responsible for the defence of the realm, but while merchants were becoming more prosperous, the income from his royal estates had remained unchanged with diminishing purchasing power during a period of rising costs. When it was necessary to strengthen the navy, and the resources of the Crown were insufficient for a national emergency, it had been customary to exact "ship-money" from ports and maritime counties. "Tunnage and poundage", or customs duties, were resisted by Parliament and made the price for concessions Charles would not grant. Having met with more opposition than he could brook, the king dispensed with Parliament from 1629 to 1640; for this reason, his demand for ship-money was regarded as unconstitutional, especially when he insisted on levying it from the moneyed classes throughout the country. Today the view that all should be taxed according to their means for a country's defence seems just and unexceptionable, but when a wealthy landowner like Hampden resisted Charles I's demands he soon became a popular hero and bulwark against tyranny, more especially as the Star Chamber had become notorious for using its power to exact heavy fines to keep the king independent of Parliament. The Star Chamber court was composed largely of Privy Councillors.

It was in religious matters, however, that the most widespread and violent antagonism to the king's cause was roused. In the reign of Henry VIII the country had accepted one Protestant Church, sanctioned by the State with supreme authority vested in the Crown. In the reigns of Mary Tudor and Queen Elizabeth a bitter and bloody struggle between Protestants and Catholics developed, to the eventual discomfiture of the latter. Puritanism, especially in its extreme Calvinist form, asserted that nothing should be interposed between the individual and God. Hence many sects arose and, instead of a wise tolerance of the individual freedom which was their source and mainspring, a perfervid bigotry which generated dissension and rabid intolerance. Although the queen was a Catholic, Charles I was strongly opposed to Catholicism, but the attempt of Archbishop Laud to restore the Church of England and give it greater unity only created deep suspicion and resentment among Puritans, particularly in the

Presbyterian Church of Scotland. It was a simple matter to convince the Puritan public that Episcopalianism spelt Popery. Milton himself, "perceiving what tyranny had invaded in the Church", refused to enter the ministry.

The position was much more complex than can be indicated briefly, and much blame attaches to both sides. Passions were violent, Charles was often tactless and ill-advised, and his opponents were actuated by a strange, short-sighted mixture of democratic principles and obstinate lack of patriotism. Economic and religious differences led to war with the Scots in 1638, and for this Charles's organization and resources proved woefully inadequate. In 1640 he recalled Parliament and soon afterwards consented to the abolition of the Star Chamber and the curtailment of episcopal power. The "root and branch" party, however, demanded the abolition of bishops; an impasse was reached and civil war broke out in 1642. By 1644, thanks mainly to the crushing defeat of the Royalists at Marston Moor, where Cromwell's regular troops played a decisive part, the Parliamentarians seemed to be reasonably certain of victory. Their stronghold was London, the commercial centre of England.

To stifle opposition before the recall of Parliament, the Royalists had insisted on stringent control of printing and the licensing of all publications. This was the effect of the Star Chamber decree concerning printing, which was passed, mainly by bishops in July 1637. On the previous June 30th, Prynne, Burton, and Bastwicke had been pilloried in Palace Yard, Westminster, and had had their ears cut off for preaching against bishops and attacking them in print. From 1640, when Parliament reassembled, there had been a lull and, in the hope of appeasement, comparative freedom of the press had been allowed. All that was insisted on was that no book should be published without the name of the author. In September 1642, soon after the opening of the Civil War in England, the Puritans, who maintained control over London, closed the theatres. Stiff-necked and narrow-minded, they were bent on imposing their will on everyone; unfortunately they were at loggerheads among themselves on both religious tenets and political aims. A great fear arose that freedom of discussion would breed "new heresies", libel and sedition; and it was in this atmosphere of distrust that Parliament passed its own Licensing Act for the censorship of the press in June 1643. To Milton it seemed that "this project of licensing crept out of the Inquisition, was caught up by our prelates, and hath caught some of our presbyters". It was virtually a complete resurrection of the old Star Chamber decree. The intolerance of the Presbyterians was to match that of the Episcopal-ians, and Milton's fears were to be realized —

New Presbyter is but Old Priest writ large.

Both bans affected Milton directly: he had planned *Paradise Lost* as a drama; and he was now a thorn in the flesh of the Parliamentarian party through publishing, without licence and without the printer's name, a pamphlet proclaiming the heretical doctrine of divorce.

WHY MILTON OPPOSED THE ACT OF 1643

Milton's reasons for writing *Areopagitica* were therefore personal as well as altruistic and liberal. In 1643 this unworldly and high-minded Parliamentarian scholar and poet had suddenly married Mary Powell, a girl of seventeen, daughter of Richard Powell of Forest Hill near Oxford. The Powells were Royalists and their property was mortgaged to the Miltons. At this time Royalist supporters were more doubtful about the victory of their party than they had been at the outset of the war, and there is little doubt that the girl Mary was used by her parents for taking out what amounted to an insurance policy for life and property. The marriage broke down almost at once and Mrs. Milton rejoined her family, not to return until after the virtually final defeat of the Royalists at the battle of Naseby, when the Powells found it provident to be on good terms with a lead-ing Parliamentarian writer. Whatever affected Milton intimately roused him deeply and the result was the hurried compilation of a pamphlet, *The Doctrine and Discipline of Divorce,* the first edition of which was published anonymously, the second with the author's name. Episcopalians were delighted to see dissension in the enemy's camp, and Presbyterians were scandalized. The Company of Sta-tioners protested and the Commons, to whom the second edition was daringly dedicated, referred the matter back to the committee set up to deal with printing. There it remained while Milton prepared his *Areopagitica* in defence of the freedom of the press. How far the poet and pamphleteer was parting company with the narrowest of the many Puritan sects may be gauged from a sonnet he wrote in 1645 after the publication of *Tetrachordon,* his third pamphlet in defence of divorce—

I did but prompt the age to quit their clogs
  By the known rules of ancient liberty,
  When straight a barbarous noise environs me
  Of owls and cuckoos, asses, apes and dogs:
As when those hinds that were transformed to frogs
  Railed at Latona's twin-born progeny,
  Which after held the sun and moon in fee.

> But this is got by casting pearl to hogs;
> That bawl for freedom in their senseless mood,
> And still revolt when truth would set them free.
> Licence they mean when they cry Liberty;
> For who loves that, must first be wise and good;
> But from that mark how far they rove we see,
> For all this waste of wealth, and loss of blood.

The personal interests of Milton in his championship of liberty must not be allowed to derogate from his general convictions. He tells us that many liberal-minded men had pressed him to use all his resources to resist "tyranny of learning"; and, to judge from the following passage from his *Second Defence of the People of England* (1654), Milton was so wholly dedicated to the cause of freedom that it is doubtful whether a more powerful and inspiring writer could have been found for the task—

"Then pursuing my former route through France, I returned to my native country, after an absence of one year and about three months; at the time when Charles, having broken the peace, was renewing what is called the episcopal war with the Scots, in which the royalists being routed in the first encounter, and the English being universally and justly disaffected, the necessity of his affairs at last obliged him to convene a parliament. As soon as I was able, I hired a spacious house in the city for myself and my books; where I again with rapture renewed my literary pursuits, and where I calmly awaited the issue of the contest, which I trusted to the wise conduct of Providence, and to the courage of the people. The vigour of the parliament had begun to humble the pride of the bishops. As long as the liberty of speech was no longer subject to control, all mouths began to be opened against the bishops; some complained of the vices of the individuals, others of those of the order. They said that it was unjust that they alone should differ from the model of other reformed churches; that the government of the church should be according to the pattern of other churches, and particularly the Word of God. This awakened all my attention and my zeal. I saw that a way was opening for the establishment of real liberty; that the foundation was laying for the deliverance of man from the yoke of slavery and superstition; that the principles of religion, which were the first objects of our care, would exert a salutary influence on the manners and constitution of the republic; and as I had from my youth studied the distinctions between religious and civil rights, I perceived that if I ever wished to be of use, I ought at least not to be wanting to my country, to the church, and to so many of my fellow-Christians, in a crisis of so much danger; I therefore determined to relinquish the other pursuits in which I was engaged, and to transfer the whole force of my talents and my industry to this one important object. I accordingly wrote two books to a friend concerning the reformation of the Church of England. Afterwards, when two bishops of superior distinction vindicated their privileges against some principal ministers, I thought that on those topics, to the consideration of which I was led solely by my love of truth, and my reverence for Christianity, I should not probably write worse than those who were contending only for their own emoluments and usurpations. I therefore answered the one in two books, of which the first is inscribed, 'Concerning Prelatical Episcopacy', and the other 'Concerning the Mode of Ecclesiastical Government'; and I replied to the other in some 'Animadversions', and soon after in an 'Apology'. On this occasion it was supposed that I brought a timely succour to the ministers, who were hardly a match for the eloquence of their opponents; and from that time I was actively employed in refuting any answers that appeared. When the bishops could no longer resist the multitude of their assailants, I had leisure to turn my thoughts to other subjects; to the promotion of real and substantial liberty; which is rather to be sought from within than from without; and whose existence depends, not so much on the terror of the sword, as on sobriety of conduct and integrity of life. When, therefore, I perceived that there were three species of liberty which are essential to the happiness of social life — religious, domestic, and civil; and as I had already written concerning the first, and the magistrates were strenuously active in obtaining the third, I determined to turn my attention to the second, or the domestic species. As this seemed to involve three material questions, the conditions of the conjugal tie, the education of the children, and the free publication of the thoughts, I made them objects of distinct consideration. I explained my sentiments, not only concerning the solemnisation of the marriage, but the dissolution, if circumstances rendered it necessary . . . I then discussed the principles of education in a summary manner, but sufficiently copious for those who attend seriously to the subject; then which nothing can be more necessary to principle the minds of men in virtue, the only genuine source of political and individual liberty, the only true safeguard of states, the bulwark of their prosperity and renown. Lastly, I wrote my 'Areopagitica', in order to deliver the press from the restraints with which it was encumbered; that the power of determining what was true and what was false, what ought to be published and what to be suppressed, might no longer be entrusted to a few illiterate and illiberal individuals, who refused their sanction to any work which contained views or sentiments at all above the level of the vulgar superstition."

To Milton the revolution in its early phases was God's will. He felt it was his mission to abandon his projected tour of Greece and return from Italy to play his part in the establishment of a kingdom of heaven on earth, the realization of which would herald the second coming of Christ. In his *Reformation Touching Church-Discipline in England* (1641), this joyful expectation raises him to a high pitch of lyrical fervour—

"Then, amidst the hymns and hallelujahs of saints, someone may perhaps be heard offering at high strains in new and lofty measures to sing and celebrate thy divine mercies and marvellous judgments in this land throughout all ages; whereby this great and warlike nation, instructed and inured to the fervent and continual practice of truth and righteousness, and casting from her the rags of her old vices, may press on hard to that high and happy emulation to be found the soberest, wisest and most Christian people at that day, when thou, the eternal and shortly expected King, shalt open the clouds to judge the several kingdoms of the world . . . "

Milton can praise neither "a fugitive and cloistered virtue" nor an "obedient unanimity" which will "starch" us all into conformity, for "truth is strong next to the Almighty" and will overcome falsehood and evil. The "unfrocking of a priest, the unmitring of a bishop, and the removing him from off the Presbyterian shoulders" are only a beginning, if "some new and great period in (God's) Church, even to the reforming of Reformation itself" is to set in. "Licensing prohibitions" must therefore not be allowed "to stand at every place of opportunity forbidding and disturbing them that continue seeking" Truth, "which came once into the world with her divine Master" and will not be wholly revealed again until his second coming.

EFFECT OF AREOPAGITICA

Milton's appeal for freedom of the press fell on deaf ears in 1644. One tyranny had been substituted for another, and no relaxation was felt to be possible until the Independents had secured power. Roman Catholic publications and Episcopalian worship were banned. The Protectorate governed by force and dared not permit freedom of political expression. In 1653 it was made illegal to print any public news without the approval of the Secretary of State. With the Restoration in 1660, positions were reversed and it was even proposed that the Star Chamber should be revived. The Licensing Act of 1662 was as stringent as ever. It was renewed until after the "bloodless revolution" of 1688-9, when constitutional government was accepted. As growing confidence returned, the law, which had been re-enacted again for a further space of two years, was allowed to pass out of existence for ever. The significance of its lapse was scarcely noticed, and it is hard to imagine the attainment of a more momentous victory, fifty years after Milton's onslaught, with such remarkable lack of publicity. By it, in the words of Macaulay, "English literature was emancipated, and emancipated for ever, from the control of the Government". The claim is not quite correct: plays still have to be licensed by the Lord Chamberlain (just as the modern film must be approved by the Censor) and newspapers, whatever the law, remained under severe political restraints until the early part of the nineteenth century.

Though it failed to achieve immediate success *Areopagitica* undoubtedly exerted a profound influence on many intellectuals who directly or indirectly promoted the happy issue of 1694. It remains the classic work on the freedom of the press. Its influence has been felt, and will continue to be felt, in many countries. It is one of those books that "are as lively, and as vigorously productive, as those fabulous dragon's teeth; and being sown up and down, may chance to spring up armed men".

SPECIAL FEATURES OF MILTON'S OUTLOOK IN AREOPAGITICA

1. Milton was no narrow-minded Puritan, unless a belief in the Wordsworthian principles of "plain living and high thinking" constitutes such narrow-mindedness. He was more in accord with the spirit of the Greeks (cf. his sonnets *To Mr. Lawrence* and *To Cyriac Skinner*) and believed in moderation inspired by reason. It was for their fanatical lack of moderation that Milton parted company with the schismatics of the 1640s. They were fiercely bigoted and intolerant, lacking the grace and flexibility of mind that Milton (and Matthew Arnold) admired in the Greeks. Their nonconformity was stiff-necked and "starched", bent on "root and branch" uniformity, inimical to truth and progress. It is by no means one of the least, though one of the last, of Milton's pleas that God "sees not as man sees, chooses not as man chooses" and that the Chapel of Westminster may be as harmful as Convocation and fail "to edify the meanest Christian, who desires to walk in the spirit and not in the letter of human trust".

2. His ideas on toleration were advanced for an age when priests sought power to suppress presbyters and presbyters were only too ready to retaliate: "if some who but of late were little better than silenced from preaching, shall come now to silence us from reading, except what they please, it cannot be guessed what is intended by some but a second tyranny over learning; and it will soon put it out of controversy that Bishops and Presbyters are the same to us both name and thing". That Milton was not ready to tolerate "Popery and open superstition", though inconsistent with his general argument, is not suprising when it is remembered that the nation had only recently succeeded in freeing itself from such a bondage. It is as if one would expect a country that had just succeeded in freeing itself from Fascist or Communist slavery to tolerate internal assaults against its freedom before it had attained sufficient maturity and confidence in itself to withstand their propaganda.

3. With this proviso, Milton believed that truth should be tolerated, however unorthodox: "Give me the liberty to know, to utter, and to argue freely according to conscience, above all liberties". It is "strong next to God" and will ultimately prevail. Though conceived in a more Christian and Biblical Spirit, Milton's ideas on toleration and progress are akin to Shelley's in *A Defence of Poetry* and Shaw's in his Preface to *St. Joan*.

4. The liberty Milton aimed at was "rational" and "strenuous". Perhaps it was for this reason that he saw a strong parallel between

his cause and that of Isocrates. He demands it only for a "mature" people, "at ripe years". To license the press is to treat the people as if they were schoolchildren: "God uses not to captivate under a perpetual childhood of prescription, but trusts him with the gift of reason to be his own chooser". Lord Hugh Cecil said in 1909, "Virtue is attained in proportion as liberty is attained: for virtue does not consist in doing right, but in choosing to do right". In his *Second Defence* Milton wrote as follows: "You, therefore, who wish to remain free, either instantly be wise, or, as soon as possible, cease to be fools; if you think slavery an intolerable evil, learn obedience to reason and the government of yourselves; and finally bid adieu to your dissensions, your jealousies, your superstitions, your outrages, your rapine, and your lusts. Unless you will spare no pains to effect this, you must be judged unfit, both by God and mankind, to be entrusted with liberty and the administration of the government, but will rather, like a nation in a state of pupilage, want some active and courageous guardian to undertake the management of your affairs." Here we have the theme of *Paradise Lost*: "Many there be that complain of divine Providence for suffering Adam to transgress. Foolish tongues! When God gave him reason, he gave him freedom to choose, for reason is but choosing". Liberty in the cause of truth is Milton's grand theme; he states that the aim of education is to repair the ruin of our parents by regaining to know God aright, and the theme is heard in harmonious verse and prose from *At a Solemn Music* to *Paradise Regained*.

5.   It is clear that Milton's insistence on freedom of choice through "reason" places him far apart from the Calvinists, who, though like Milton most hotly opposed to the Episcopal Church of Laud, believed in predestination.

6.   At the time of writing *Areopagitica,* Milton was sublimely optimistic. In this he is comparable to other political poets: to Wordsworth in the first flush of enthusiasm for the French Revolution when France seemed to be "standing on the top of golden hours"—

> Bliss was it in that dawn to be alive,
> But to be young was very Heaven!

or to Shelley at the outbreak of the struggle for Greek Independence—

> The world's great age begins anew,
> The golden years return . . .

Milton had supreme faith in the vitality of England: "Methinks I see in my mind a noble and puissant nation rousing herself like a strong man after sleep, and shaking her invincible locks. Methinks I see her as an eagle muing her mighty youth, and kindling her undazzled eyes at the full midday beam; purging and unsealing her long-abused sight at the fountain itself of heavenly radiance . . ." Here was a people ripe for truth and liberty. England had accomplished what Rome had failed to do. She had been chosen by God "that out of her as out of Sion should be proclaimed and sounded forth the first tidings and trumpet of Reformation to all Europe", and now it was her mission "to begin some great period in His Church, even to the reforming of Reformation itself." Milton's vision is Messianic; the reforming of the Reformation would prepare the way for the Master's second coming. The kingdom of heaven was near: "We reckon more than five months to harvest; there need not be five weeks; had we but eyes to lift up, the fields are white already".

7. Milton's thoughts are frequently conceived in the imagery of "our sage and serious poet Spenser". In a Latin poem addressed in Italy to the aged literary patron Manso, Milton mentions themes which he hoped would be the subject of his poetry on his return to England. One of these concerned King Arthur, and is a type of those that later appealed to Wordsworth—

> Whence inspiration for a song that winds
> Through ever-changing scenes of votive quest
> Wrongs to redress, harmonious tribute paid
> To patient courage and unblemished truth . . .
>
> (*The Prelude* I, cf. ll. 166-185).

There is little doubt that Milton when he writes of Truth grappling with Falsehood is harking back to the chivalric allegories of *The Faerie Queene*.

HINTS ON THE STYLE

It is not likely that Milton had an eye on posterity when he wrote his pamphlets. He was engaged in polemics, and his supreme purpose was to convince contemporaries and not to court posthumous fame. In poetry it was different. In nearly all his poems he aimed at perfection and permanence; they are "the precious life-blood of a master spirit, embalmed and treasured up on purpose to a life beyond life". Milton was less at home with English prose and admitted that in writing it it was as if he had but the use of his left hand. It was "with small willingness" that he left a "calm and pleasing solitariness . . . to embark in a troubled sea of noises and hoarse disputes".

Areopagitica, however, suffers less from topicality than most of Milton's prose. Often when the controversy is restricted in time and place to the originating dispute and its factions, the prose is clogged; the more the theme approaches universality of truth, the more freely and lucidly it flows. In general, the prose is improvised and inspirational. Its unevenness registers the degree of harmony between the writer and the various aspects and developments of his subject. Calculated elegances are brief and incidental. Milton has difficulty in getting under way because idealizations are obfuscated by personal involvements to which he cannot even allude, and the flattery which tactfully follows is somewhat forced. On books or the subject of temptation or religion or the unity of spirit which he yearns for in the nation, his thought is unequivocal and his expression untrammelled. We hear Milton's voice.

For Milton is speaking; he imagines that he is addressing the High Court of Parliament and his style is oratorical in the classical tradition. The occasion may be lost sight of, but we are reminded of it repeatedly. In that noble passage on the pursuit of the scattered fragments of Truth, he writes: "We have not found them all, Lords and Commons, nor ever shall do, till her Master's second coming . . .". He appeals to them to have faith in the country's capacity to discern reason: "Lords and Commons of England, consider what nation it is whereof ye are, and whereof ye are the governors . . ." and he reminds them of the wise exhortations of one of their leaders: "I only shall repeat what I have learnt from one of your own honourable number . . . Ye know him I am sure; yet I for honour's sake, and may it be eternal to him, shall name him, the Lord Brooke". He indulges in rhetorical flourishes: "There be, who knows not there be . . .". We hear dra-, matic pauses and emphases, as at the climax to a typically inspired argument: " . . . when all the faith and religion that shall be there canonized, is not sufficient . . . to edify the meanest Christian, who desires to walk in the Spirit, and not in the letter of human trust, for all the number of voices that can be there made; no, though Harry the VII himself there, with all his liege tombs about him, should lend them voices from the dead, to swell their number". Occasionally, he uses the time-honoured rhetorical device of repetition to fortify his argument. Changes of tone express varying emotions, as he works subtly on his audience; note, for example, the quiet neutrality with which he opens an argument, then cultivates a receptive mood through humour and idiom, to turn swiftly into fluent and engaging banter, and conclude with the most terse and withering sarcasm. The whole paragraph is a masterpiece of oratory, which would have "wrung the withers" of the Parliamentarians, had they been listening.

This does not imply that the whole of *Areopagitica* would have been an excellent speech. The style suffers from classical constructions and is often laborious. Milton's scholarship is sometimes, especially in the early historical section, so weighty and unalleviated that he cannot soar; he is no more than pedestrian.

Yet at his best, and there are many such passages, he combines scholarship and plain simple English with marked felicity and fluency. The Bible is as much the source of his main inspiration as are Greek and Latin authors. The range of his knowledge and expression is wide.

His style is commonly "double-plated". Almost any paragraph will illústrate his recurrent use of adjectives, nouns or verbs in pairs, occasionally varied with the triplicate form (a characteristic of Samuel Johnson). Alliteration, in which his master Spenser was fecund, adds force, e.g. "laziness of a licensing Church", the Pope with his appurtenances the prelates", "in a peculiar manner propitious and propending towards us". Epigrammatic expression provides occasional punch: "the reforming of Reformation itself", "suppress the suppressors", "liberty which is the nurse of all great wits", "our richest merchandise, Truth", "Bishops and Presbyters are the same to us both name and thing".

His mood is variable. Papacy and "starched" conformity provoke his spleen. The possibilities of a glorious future arouse lyrical enthusiasm. Sometimes he reasons without passion; sometimes he pleads gently and patiently. Occasionally he is amused and high spirits express themselves not only, as we have seen, in ironical banter but also in word-jugglery, which he finds irresistible. "Conceits", puns and quibbles were fashionable in Elizabethan and post-Elizabethan literature. The word-play of *Areopagitica* extends from the most scholarly (*e.g.* "enchiridion") to the most obvious (*e.g.* "Star Chamber decree . . . Court . . . fallen from the stars with Lucifer").

The pamphleteers of Milton's period were not sparing in invective or abuse, and Milton was no exception. His powers of vituperation in some of his pamphlets are astonishing both in extent and coarseness, and have occasioned embarrassment in some admirers of the author of *Paradise Lost*. No give-and-take was possible, however, in religious and political propaganda, and the ferocity and vulgarity of the exchanges are a reflex of the bid for victory and of the powerful, Zeal-of-the-Lord, contempt and hatred engendered by sectarians in an age of desperate struggles for power. Passionate animosities are expressed in *Areopagitica,* but fortunately it is almost wholly free from the unpleasant abusiveness characteristic of the polemical writings of the period. It is sustained by lofty principles expressed in equally lofty prose of impassioned magniloquence. The style may be dated, but the principles are universally true (though not applied), and for this reason the work remains a "classic" as significant to-day as it was in the seventeenth century.

Milton's imagination is visual and much of the splendour of the *Areopagitica* resides in the imagery. This imagery sometimes consists of direct description as in the picture of the comfortable parochial minister, though here it is the associated image ("at his Hercules pillars in a warm benefice"), containing the central idea, which is most impressive. The concluding pictorial parallelism, which illustrates the stratagem used to defend this worthy from heresy and schism, is comparable to that of many other passages and an example of the more elaborate "conceits" to be found in sixteenth and seventeenth century authors. For the most part Milton uses imagery to express ideas, whether briefly as in "the ghost of a linen decency" or in extension as in the matchless picture of middle-class merchant Pharisaism. The most splendid imagery is in the oft-quoted passage, "Methinks I see in my mind a noble and puissant nation . . .", where Milton imagines the might of England as the reviving Samson or as an eagle "kindling her undazzled eyes at the midday beam". The sun as a symbol of Truth is recurrent, but one of the most elaborate images on this subject is that of Osiris, in a passage which is both magnificently conceived and expressed. For intensiveness of thought in imagery, few passages are comparable with that on books. Abstract the ideas, and it will be seen how much is due to the vividness of Milton's concrete apprehension. The imagery conforms to the subject. Here, in ridicule of licensing, is a picture of the author who is allowed publication: he "must appear in print like a puny with his guardian and his censor's hand on the back of his title to be his bail and surety, that he is no idiot or seducer . . .".

Milton appeals both to the eye and ear of the imagination, and it is therefore advisable, once their meaning and dramatic appeal have been generally understood, that passages should be read aloud if all the intended effects are to be realized.

Of course Milton is partial to the "periodic" style, *e.g.* the passages beginning "First, when a city shall be as it were besieged" and "When a man hath been labouring the hardest labour in the deep mines of knowledge"; but to classify his prose as periodic is an injustice. A study of the sequel to the second passage reveals ample variety of sentence-construction. Unlike Samuel Johnson, Milton did not cultivate a few arts of style, which become monotonous by repetition. As a writer, he luxuriated in the copiousness of the most fertile

Elizabethan writers, but his style is never tenuous or long drawn out. It is masculine and expresses the pressure of a master-mind; no words are wasted, and there are times when ellipsis or contraction seems an excessive abnegation to the modern reader. Exuberance of idea and expression drives Milton on with such momentum that at times he cannot restrain himself, and in the midst of a "paragraph" (which comprises nearly a quarter of the whole work!) he is swept forward into the next section of his address, having already anticipated his argument: "See the ingenuity of Truth, who when she gets a free and willing hand, opens herself faster than the pace of method and discourse can overtake her". His prose is like a stream that is infinitely varied in its course: sometimes in torrential flood as it sweeps aside all impediments, with difficulty or glorious ease; now turbid, now limpid, under frowning, grey or radiant skies; here achieving magnificent sonority, and there, along level reaches, murmuring of spiritual charity and peace.

PUNCTUATION

One feature of the composition of *Areopagitica* which readers may find perplexing is the punctuation. Within the sentence Milton has only three stops at his command: the comma, the semi-colon and the colon. These often function in the orthodox modern fashion, but Milton uses them for a variety of purposes; for example, a brief aside may be indicated by commas, and a longer one or a passage of direct speech may be introduced by a colon.

Another use calls for special attention. The style of *Areopagitica* is oratorical, and Milton uses commas, semi-colons and colons to indicate pauses of varying length in imaginary speech in much the same way as Shakespeare had employed them in drama. Sometimes they occur where the sense does not demand them; a simple example is afforded by the comma. The concluding sentence of the first paragraph provides an apt illustration of the oratorical use of other stops.

If *Areopagitica* is read as spoken language, little difficulty will be experienced with the original text. Its punctuation is far more satisfactory than that of relatively modern variants, and it. has been liberally used as a corrective in this edition. Even so, there are points where the punctuation is clearly invalid or doubtful, (where an involved periodic sentence introducing a completely new thought appears as a lengthy appendage curiously attached to two statements which form an independent whole). It is impossible to say whether such *errata* arise from the inadvertence of printers or from Milton's precipitance in writing and securing illicit publication.

SUMMARY

PREFACE

Addressing the High Court of Parliament, Milton states that his main emotion derives from the prospect of the joy his appeal will bring to all who seek their country's liberty. The greatest liberty that can be expected is reached "when complaints are freely heard, deeply considered, and speedily reformed". England, thanks to God and Parliament, has already gone far towards achieving this. His integrity is shown by the fact that his praise is linked with criticism. The Lords and Commons are enlightened like the Greeks, and he appeals to them in the manner of Isocrates. He asks them to reconsider their Orders for the Regulation of Printing, and enumerates the four parts of his appeal.

I. The originators of licensing are those with whom they will be loth to be associated

Milton admits there must be a restricted censorship, but urges great restraint. In Athens only blasphemous and libellous books were burned or expurgated. So with the Romans, until tyranny crept in; and in the early Christian era until Papal influence predominated. Papal practice had lately commended itself to the Episcopal Church of England, and surely Parliament cannot sympathise with Prelacy.

II. On the value of reading without restrictions

If such was the origin of licensing, it is difficult to see its value. Moses, Daniel, and Paul were widely read, and it seemed to the persecutors of the early Christians that the best way of destroying Christianity was to prevent its leaders from studying heathen literature. To the pure, all things are pure. Mr. Selden, a distinguished member of Parliament, is a leading supporter of the view that the speediest way to truth is through the consideration of all opinions, including those that have been condemned. Every mature person must judge for himself; God has endowed us with reason for no other purpose. This is the lesson of the Fall; only by trial and error, shall we learn truth and goodness.

The alleged harm of books falls into three kinds:

(1) They may spread infection. If this were so, the Bible would have to be withdrawn. If it is answered that the danger from foreign books is not great, it must be remembered that the least principled man may be scholarly enough to read them; in fact, in religion, the harm is more likely to derive from scholars than from the general public. It can spread without books. To suppress all learning from

books would be too great a price to pay. Moreover, if learned men can err, licensers will not be infallible. We must not handicap the wise for fear of fools.

(2) People should not be exposed to temptation unnecessarily.

(3) We should not waste time on "vain things".

The answer to the last two objections has already been given: true virtue (strength and purity) comes from resisting temptation.

III. Licensing does not suppress scandalous, seditious and libellous books

No nation or well instituted state that valued books ever resorted to this device. Plato's licensing was for an imaginary Commonwealth and not at all in keeping with the width of his own reading. To regulate morals, it would be necessary to control all recreations and pastimes, music, food and drink, clothing, and personal friendships and associations. This is impossible, and we must ordain wisely for a world of evil, not for Utopias. God gave us reason to choose between good and evil. Virtue cannot exist without sin and temptation. In any event, such an order would be ignored. Unlawful books would have to be withdrawn; other books would have to be expurgated. Even if this were done, heresies and schisms could not be prevented, and it is quite impossible to find licensers of sufficient learning and integrity to submit to the sustained drudgery that licensing would demand.

IV. The harmful effect of the Licensing Act in hindering the pursuit of knowledge and truth

How can learned men submit to tyranny and distrust? Should considered judgments be submitted to inferiors? How can books be expanded or amended before printing if every alteration necessitates a further degrading and inconvenient visit to the Licenser? Only conventional views will be accepted, and earlier books will be edited to conform. If such censoring obtained, ignorance would be bliss. Such a measure is discreditable to the nation. It is impossible that everyone's views can be comprehended by twenty licensers or that people can submit to such servitude. What a reflection on the incapacity of the Church! Milton had learnt from his travels that England was regarded as the home of liberty, but now it looks as if the Presbyterian Church is to be as narrow and tyrannical as the Episcopal. Repression will increase sects and schisms. It is possible to be heretical or superstitious by merely accepting old orthodoxies. Conformity will produce sham respectability in the public and torpor in the Church. What can be sounder for a country's welfare than that great thinkers should be free to voice their opinions publicly? The neglect of their churches by the priests fully occupied with licensing is a matter of trivial importance compared with the retardation of progress this Act would cause.

Truth will not be fully revealed until our Lord's second coming, but in the meantime we cannot "pitch our tent". We must use the light of knowledge to seek further knowledge. England has long been held in high repute for her learning, and was chosen to herald Reformation throughout Europe. The time has now come for further reforms. The industry of scholars and thinkers in London could not be greater, and yet this order would suppress many of them as schismatics. It should be realized that a young and vigorous nation at a critical period will put forward many different views on the best way to achieve progress. Liberty "is the nurse of all great wits" and truth should be given every opportunity to prevail. It is "strong next to the Almighty", but may not appear the same to all, though the differences are likely to be superficial if men are actuated by the right motives. Popery, superstition, impiety and evil should not be tolerated after every effort has been made to "regain the weak and misled". Truth is the first victim when licensing is introduced. When God stirs a kingdom to reform he raises men of rare ability and uncommon industry for his work. God, however, does not see as we see. If our leaders appear wrong, they should be refuted publicly; if, on the other hand, it happens that God's chosen are suppressed by the licensing of the press, so much the worse for the country.

CONCLUSION

It is to be hoped that none of those who have published unlicensed books for the enlightenment of the public will support this Act. The suppressors should be suppressed, if they cannot be restrained. The only necessary printing regulation was contained in the previous Order. That of 1643 derives from the Inquisition and is almost identical with the infamous Star Chamber decree of 1637. Possibly it was passed to favour certain publishers. Any Government may make mistakes, but speedy amends may be expected from a Parliament which has proved itself capable of "highest actions".

QUESTIONS ON STYLE

1. Find examples of words used with Latin or Greek connotations (*e.g.* excremental, municipal, conversation) and show from their contexts how Milton uses them.

2. Illustrate Milton's use of alliteration and find expressions which are partially or wholly epigrammatic.

3. Illustrate the oratorical characteristics of *Areopagitica*.

4. Find passages which appear cumbrous or awkward.

5. Select contrasting passages to show magniloquence of style and fluent simplicity of diction.

6. Show how Milton expresses ideas through imagery.

7. Illustrate Milton's use of flattery and irony.

8. Consider the style of Swift in *Gulliver's Travels* and discuss (a) the gain, (b) the loss, if *Areopagitica* had been written in this style.

GENERAL QUESTIONS

1. What are Milton's main arguments for the freedom of the press?

2. What is required of a nation by Milton if it warrants freedom of the press? Would he have made such freedom unlimited?

3. What does Milton say on Plato, Selden, Spenser, Adam, Galileo?

4. Does *Areopagitica* suggest that Milton was a Puritan?

5. To what extent does Areopagitica provide a commentary on Thomas Huxley's dictum that "new truths begin as heresies and end as superstitions"?

6. How far does *Areopagitica* show that Milton was an idealist and a realist?

7. Relate the argument of *Areopagitica* to *Comus* and *Paradise Lost*.

8. To what extent is Milton's character revealed in *Areopagitica?*

THE TENURE OF KINGS AND MAGISTRATES

In this document Milton realizes that compromise with King Charles is impossible, and, when Charles was put on trial, Milton was one of those who deemed it advisable and just to depose him and put him to death. This work was intended to silence those who opposed the plans of the Presbyterians to kill Charles; it appeared only two weeks after the execution of the king. Perhaps it was this work which helped him become Secretary in the government.

Milton argues that men are naturally free, and that all contracts with rulers are voluntary, and therefore can be broken whenever men wished it so. The people have a perfect right to depose a ruler found tyrannical; the right extends even to extreme measures of death, if such measures will help the progress of the state. Nowhere does Milton mention Charles by name, although the allusion is obvious. To buttress his arguments Milton quotes authorities from the classical writers, the Church Fathers, political writers of modern times, even Scripture, all proving the right of the people to depose and kill tyrants. His political thinking is consonant with that of most of the Renaissance writers, and nothing is said that has not often been discussed before. The work is written in a clear, plain style, rather than in the impassioned vein of much of his other political writing.

EIKONOKLASTES

In February, 1649, there appeared, in twenty-eight parts, a famous King's Book, *Eiken Basilike,* which was a kind of autobiography of Charles I, designed to stir up the people in favor of the good, pious monarch. The subtitle, *The True Portraiture of His Sacred Majesty in His Solitudes and Sufferings,* is an indication of the tone of the work. In it are given the self-meditations of the conscientious family man, who loved his country and God. It was not Charles, of course, but probably a Dr. John Gauden, who wrote this hoax, in an attempt to make a saint and martyr of the king. The leaders of the Commonwealth considered it a dangerous work and asked Milton to refute it.

Milton answers the charges of the work paragraph by paragraph. *Eikonoklastes* means image-breakers. Milton carefully, if boringly, tries to prove the falsity of Charles' defence of his actions. He condemns the king on every point, especially on his hypocrisy in trying to appear pious in order to conceal his tyrannical ambition and designs. A certain prayer offered by Charles he proves had been plagiarized from Sidney's *Arcadia.* Some of the sources that aided Milton in this work are Thomas Mory's *History of Parliament* (1647) and *Eiken Alethine* (1649), an anonymous work.

THE DEFENSE OF THE ENGLISH PEOPLE AGAINST SALMASIUS

This political tract (the title is translated from the Latin) was occasioned by a work by Salmasius, or Claude Saumaise, who, upon the request of Charles II, attempted to defend Charles I and condemn the new government that had executed him. Salmasius was a French scholar who wrote his work in Latin, entitling it *Defensio Regis pro Carole I.* Again, the effect of this book was considered dangerous, especially when it was written by a leading international scholar of great repute. As usual, it was Milton's task to refute the charges, and hence the appearance of this tract.

Milton wrote in Latin, not only because Salmasius did, but also because he was addressing all of Europe, and not just the English. Milton, rather mistakenly, called this prose effect a "noble task" that had set all of Europe to talking. To us, today, it does not appear to be very praiseworthy. Salmasius is abused without cease, and in the abuse of personalities, the main argument is often lost sight of. Again Milton cities authorities to buttress his arguments on the necessity and the legal right of regicide. Most of the arguments and authorities are repetitions of the same in his previous works. This work did effect, however, the dismissal of Salmasius from Queen Christian's Swedish Court. It also caused Milton's sight to be impaired beyond recovery.

THE SECOND DEFENCE FOR THE PEOPLE OF ENGLAND

This work also was a reply to another, an anonymous publication called *The Cry of the King's Blood to Heaven Against the English Parricides,* written in Latin. Milton, also writing in Latin, attacked Alexander More or Morus as the author, although the real author was probably Peter Du Moulin. Again, the abuse levelled on the supposed author is vicious and crude, but we must remember that in those days personal abuse was more or less expected in the stress and strain of war and peace. The rest of the work, however, is a finer attempt than the *First Defense.* It praises and defends the new leaders of the Commonwealth and in it abound patriotic devotion and an enthusiasm for real freedom. The style is eloquent and impassioned, especially in the apotheosis of Cromwell and in passages that tell of Milton's own lifelong services to the state. Milton is anxious to clear himself of all the vicious charges brought against him, and the result is a wonderful autobiographical fragment. At the start, Milton gives us an inkling that he is far from devoid of a sort of grim humor, when, twitted by Salmasius on his loss of sight and ugliness, he says: "I certainly never supposed that I should have been obliged to enter into a competition for beauty with the Cyclops," then goes on to defend himself against this personal slander, saying he is of middle stature, never known to have any deformity, and exercised with the broadsword constantly in youth. His blindness is nothing to be ashamed of, and he is not conscious of committing any wrong which could call for this blindness as a *punishment.* He relates the circumstances leading to his blindness, the defense of the cause of his state; and he prefers his blindness to that of his antagonist.

With his usual stoicism, Milton says that there is a way to strength through weakness, and that he has been blessed by God. He now gives a brief biography of himself; his father was distinguished by integrity in life, and his mother by charity. As a boy he studied until midnight, although his eyes were weak. He mentions graduation, his period at Horton, which he spent in study, his Italian trip, the meetings with such noblemen as Gaddi and Manso, stressing the constant friendship that was shown him both here and at College. Then comes his return home, his defense of reformed religion against Catholicism, etc. Through it all runs the pathos of Milton's blindness, his sincerity, his earnestness, his pride in himself, his courage, idealism, etc. This idealism takes form in calling the English people to maintain liberty and justice.

A TREATISE OF CIVIL POWER IN ECCLESIASTICAL CAUSES

In this ecclesiastical pamphlet, Milton further aids the cause of liberty and toleration. He insisted that civil authorities had no right to force upon others certain religious beliefs. He argues for the separation of Church and State. Scripture is the only divine authority; men must interpret Scripture in the light of their own judgment; and men are certainly not infallible. It is a plea for complete toleration of any and all sects or religions, except Papistry. The Papists are excluded from toleration only because they are still politically dangerous and represent a threat to the welfare of the newly installed government.

THE READY AND EASY WAY TO ESTABLISH A FREE COMMONWEALTH

This is Milton's answer to those who believed in bringing back Charles II to head the government. The restoration of Charles II he considered a perilous step. First he goes over all the past history that had finally brought about the Commonwealth, and then he shows how everything that men had worked for would be destroyed by the return of all the evils with Charles II himself. He preferred, instead, that sovereignty should be vested in a Grand Council that should sit forever, chosen by a restricted electorate. He said forever, so that the body would impart stability and would have at its disposal the best minds of the country. Although he was against a succession of parliaments, he makes provisions for a limited rotation of members. Certainly there is no real democratic feeling here. Milton was an advocate of limited democracy, or rather, of a government ruled by a few, that few being a sort of aristocratic guardian group, similar to Plato's scheme in the Republic. Many Englishmen rightly attacked Milton's views on the subject.

THE HISTORY OF BRITAIN

When Milton was not strenuously engaged in public or civil controversies, he was busy also with works of more or less pure scholarship. He had started, but never completed, a Latin dictionary; he also worked on a *History of Britain,* and the Latin work, *Of Christian Doctrine.*

This historical work was part of Milton's earlier ambitions for the composition of something about British legend or folklore. When he rejected the Arthurian legend, in order to write the epic on the Biblical story he had not yet lessened his interest in patriotic, national history, and legend.

The History of Britain records his interest, a result as well of tremendous reading and research of the records of the Commonplace Book, the historian's Holinshed, Camden and Speed as well as Gildas and Bede, of the older school. He distrusted the manner in which British historians narrated English history, without manner or style, dignity or restraint. He wished to write history in the manner of the Roman historians, Tacitus or Sallust, or Caesar. The period covered ranges from the prehistoric origins down to the Norman Conquest. Although begun around 1645 or 1646, it was not published until 1670, a sign, perhaps, that his original aim was to bring events down to his own period in history. The *History,* therefore, must remain an uncompleted work.

Milton, in his work, aims for truth and intelligibility. He attacks those who will credulously recount all kinds of old fairy tales and legends as fact. He does include, however, those legends or tales that have gained more or less literary and historical fame. A good deal of the work censures other historians, like Geoffrey, Buchanan, and the Anglo-Saxon chroniclers, for being false, obscure, credulous, childish, and the like. He will tell "the truth naked." Unlike other historians, he does go directly to the original sources, and, like good modern historians, tries to evaluate their contribution. As a critic and scholar, he is somewhat of a pioneer in the writing of modern history. Unlike good modern historians, however, he injects into his book too much of his philosophical views. He believed, for instance, that there was a natural connection between prosperity of the nation and its morality, and he emphasizes this point with undue length.

He views history also as a guide to modern actions. History will teach us lessons. Besides, many personal prejudices, political biases, and moral enthusiasms mar the historical objectivity of the work. The history has a limited value as history, but it is interesting for a further glance into Milton's personality and mental equipment.

DE DOCTRINE CHRISTIANA, OR, THE CHRISTIAN DOCTRINE

It was not until 1823 that this work was discovered, and not until 1825 that it was published. This posthumous work was kept by Daniel Skinner, a friend, to whom it was given by Milton before his death. Skinner, however, was afraid to publish it after Milton's passing, since it contained religious ideas that might hurt his own political ambitions. The work then remained in the Public Record Office until it was discovered by the Keeper. Bishop Charles Sumner translated and edited it, and, in 1825, Macaulay was able to use its publication as a pretext for his popular essay on Milton.

When Milton first started work on the book, there were plans afoot, in the period of the Commonwealth, to unite the Protestant sects in a program of liberal Christianity. That is one reason why, in the Restoration period, when such plans were definitely hostile, the work was not considered fit for publication, with its emphasis on this unity of sects. Besides, the book was really heretic, what with its denial of the Calvinistic theory of pre-destination and its conception of the second and third persons of the Trinity. It also criticizes all worship that is not simple, and adds his views on divorce, showing that God may not have prohibited even polygamy. The work insists that man has free will; that Biblical authorities, not man's interpretations, should be followed; that the immortality of the soul is questionable.

It is the Bible that Milton delights in referring to, as part of his program of Christian belief. Only the Bible is the real authority; all deviations from Scripture are usually vicious, immoral, and irreligious in the real sense. Whether or not he will accept any doctrine is determined almost exclusively by that doctrine's agreement with the writings in the Bible. The style here is not, as usual, warm and impassioned, but cold, formal, logical. No intrusions of his personality, no eloquent effusions, mark this highly intellectual performance. It is an important document, nevertheless, and reveals to us many of his theological views, and, as such, can be used as a guide to the theological problems of the greater *Paradise Lost*.